Birnbaum on Strategy

THE GUIDE TO COST-TO-VALUE ANALYSIS

David Birnbaum
Emma Birnbaum

Published by:

FASHIONDEX, Inc.

Apparel Industry Publishers
New York, New York
www.fashiondex.com

First Printing 2020

Copyright © David Birnbaum
Copyright © The Fashiondex, Inc.

All rights reserved under International and Pan-American Copyright Conventions. No part of this book may be reproduced or transmitted in any form or by any means, electronic or mechanical, including photocopy, recording, or any information or retrieval system, without prior written permission from the publisher. Fashiondex, Inc. cannot accept responsibility for the accuracy or completeness of such information or for loss or damage caused by any use thereof.

ISBN: 978-0-9851058-7-7

Published by:

FASHIONDEX, Inc.
New York, NY 10001
U.S.A.

www.fashiondex.com
info@fashiondex.com

Also by David Birnbaum

Birnbaum is the author of the following books used as standard texts at universities and institutes:

> Birnbaum's Global Guide: Agents and Buying Offices, New York, Fashiondex, 2015.
>
> India Benchmark Study (7 Countries), New Delhi, Government of India, 2014.
>
> Crisis in the 21st Century Garment Industry and Breakthrough Unified Strategies, New York, Fashiondex, 2008.
>
> Source It: Global Material Sourcing for the Clothing Industry, International Trade Centre, Geneva, 2005.
>
> Birnbaum's Global Guide to Material Sourcing, New York, Fashiondex, 2005.
>
> Birnbaum's Garment Imports: Annual Report 2003, New York, Fashiondex, 2003.
>
> Birnbaum's Global Guide to Winning the Great Garment War, Hong Kong, 2000, sixth edition, New York, Fashiondex, 2010.
>
> Birnbaum's Directory of Garment Factories and Agents: Hong Kong & South China, Hong Kong, 1995.
>
> Importing Garments Through Hong Kong: A Guide for the Perplexed, Hong Kong, 1995

Birnbaum also writes The Birnbaum Report, a monthly newsletter for international garment industry professionals. The Report is the largest compendium of global garment trade data available. He also maintains a blog at www.birnbaumandfather.com featuring articles relating to the global garment industry as well as other general topics.

Dedication

Our global garment industry is over sixty years old. It has run its course and even now is being replaced by a new and very different global garment industry.

This is a book about change. We at Birnbaum & Father also must accept that change.

It is therefore only fitting and proper that this book is a joint effort between my daughter Emma Birnbaum and me.

This will be both my last book and at the same time Emma's first book.

This book is dedicated to those professionals who at this moment are building the new industry.

Acknowledgements

Ram Sareen: I am not a computer software specialist, nor am I at the forefront of the latest garment industry technology. Ram Sareen is one of the world's leading garment industry software specialists and his company Tukatech is at the very cutting edge of our industry's technology. I am grateful for his advice and assistance in these areas.

Josephine Bow: Non-professionals think of the editing process in terms of correct spelling, grammar and punctuation. Line editing is indeed important. However, real editing is structural – the ability to take complex ideas and multifaceted structures and bring them together in an organized form that will allow the reader to understand the material in the book. This is a long and arduous task requiring special talents involving not only writing skills but, more importantly, real industry knowledge and experience. Josephine has been my editor for over two decades during which time did she has managed to keep my writing straight. In her own right Josephine is a garment industry specialist. During our time together, she has worked with me in many projects located in over 20 countries. I can truly say that her greatest skill has been her ability to put up with me.

Table of Contents

Also by David Birnbaum	iii
Dedication	iv
Acknowledgements	v
Table of Contents	vii
Preface	ix
Introduction	xi
Book I: Tools of the Trade	
Chapter 1 Tools	3
Chapter 2 Static vs. Dynamic Cost Sheets	11
Chapter 3 Intrinsic Cost Savings	13
Chapter 4 Intrinsic Costs: Schedules and Capacity	21
Chapter 5 Extrinsic Costs	27
Chapter 6 Calculating Value of Soft Services	31
Chapter 7 Negative Value Soft Services	37
Chapter 8 Cost vs Price	41
Chapter 9 The Incomplete Cost Sheet	47
Chapter 10 Full Value Cost Sheet	53
Chapter 11 Reducing Markdowns	57
Chapter 12 The Competitive Model	63
Chapter 13 The Cooperative Model	67
Book II: Where Do You Want to Go and How Do You Get There	
Chapter 14 The Collaborative Model: Part I	73
Chapter 15 Technology I: From Analogue to Digital	79
Chapter 16 Technology II: Soft Technology Alternatives	85
Chapter 17 Technology III: The On-Demand Microfactory	89
Chapter 18 Cost-to-Value Analysis: The Ultimate Cost Sheet	97
Chapter 19 Branding the Supplier Side	101
Chapter 20 Decline of Brick and Mortar and Rise of E-Commerce	107
Chapter 21 Developing New SME E-Commerce Supplier Sector	109
Chapter 22 The Universal Factory Supplier	115
Chapter 23 Innovation	121
Chapter 24 The Customer Side	125
Chapter 25 The Space-Time Continuum	129
Book III: The Way Forward	
Chapter 26 Evolutionary Changes	137
Chapter 27 The Collaborative Model: Part II	145
Chapter 28 The Future of the Fashion Industry	153
Chapter 29 Towards the Industry Yet to Come	163
Glossary	169
Index	179

Preface

Accountant to Garmento:
Murray, your selling price for this style is less than your material cost.
How do you expect to make a profit?

Garmento to Accountant:
No problem!
I will make it back on volume.

We are third and fourth-generation garmentos. Morris Birnbaum, our second generation, operated a factory in Hong Kong during the 1950s, at the dawn of today's global garment export industry. Those were the days when made-in-Hong Kong garments were at the very bottom of the market: in my father's case, that meant men's cotton woven shirts at FOB $7.50 a dozen. (Yes, you could make money at those prices provided you bought 40-count yarn-dyed cotton fabric at 20¢ a yard and paid your worker $50 per month).

All things considered the old man ran a pretty good operation, particularly when you compare his factory in 1955 with the same factory in Bangladesh in 2020 (the world's second-largest exporter of men's cotton woven shirts). His 600 machines produced 1000 dozen a day, which was a lot higher productivity than the same guy in Bangladesh, and $50 a month in today's money is over five times what a worker in Bangladesh is paid.

There was one area where he did not do a good job: garment costings. In this regard, my father was very much old school. In his defense, let me say that in those early days, old school was probably new school or, more to the point, the only school.

Be that as it may, the Morris Birnbaum school of garment costing was based on the MONEY-IN-THE-POCKET principle. In those early days before the advent of what is known today as garment sourcing, customers still bought their garments and factories not only produced the goods, but also sourced the fabric and trim. The Birnbaum method was very simple and practical: if the fabric cost 20¢ a yard, my father's costing read 22¢; 30 yards a dozen became 33 yards a dozen. Every trim item – buttons, interlining, thread, labels – carried its own markup.

The customers, on the other hand, as represented by their own garmento marauders, were governed by the NO-BOTTOM-PRICE principle. This too was very simple. Whatever FOB price the factory quoted was unacceptable. If the factory quoted $7.00 a dozen, the garmento marauder demanded $6.50. If $6.50, the demand was for $6.00. This process continued until the true bottom price had been reached, often breaking the factory in the process.

In this highly competitive environment, the actual costing played little or no role whatsoever. In the course of negotiations my father invariably forgot the actual costs, while the customer never knew or cared about the actual cost. Eventually, my father and his generation went to that great buying-office-in-the-sky where the ultimate QC manager separates out the rejects.

Times changed. People changed. New tools, new systems and new structures evolved. The old tussling between MONEY-IN-THE POCKET and NO-BOTTOM-PRICE never completely died out. We can still see it sometimes today albeit dressed up in a suit of modern technology.

But for the most part, on both the customer and supplier sides, the industry has moved on. The third-generation following after Morris Birnbaum's MONEY-IN-THE-POCKET generation are still garmentos although operating in a very different industry. Meanwhile our fourth-generation garmento is a specialist in a garment industry still in its nascent stage which will become mainstream in a few years.

David Birnbaum
Emma Birnbaum
Birnbaum & Father Ltd.

Introduction

I am grateful to Matthias Knappe of the International Trade Centre who suggested I write this book.

Our industry is faced with a fundamental problem: The decisions we make increasingly do not provide the solutions we expect.

We blame this on incompetent management. Where once CEOs held their position for a decade or longer, their life expectancies have now been reduced to two or three years.

We blame this on our inability to keep up with an ever-changing industry. We continually search for greater data and more sophisticated data analysis to tell us what is going on in our own company.

In fact, the real problem lies with the decision-making process itself. We operate in a world where our managers are increasingly more educated with access to ever more sophisticated tools, yet most often reach their most important decisions on the old system known as LET'S-ASK-COUSIN-PHIL.

Industry today has many Cousin Phils. They may indeed be someone's cousin, a senior manager, a well-known expert or an international consultancy. What they all share in common is their ability to provide plausible solutions to every problem. Here are two exemplary case studies, the first from the customer side.

Case Study I: Pollution and the Leather Product Industry

A senior executive at a major leatherware company is concerned about consumers' ever-growing environmental concerns.

Since leather is probably the fashion industry's greatest source of pollution, the executive thinks perhaps his company might do well to take a proactive approach:

- Communicate with the end consumer
- Show that his company works with the very best tanneries in Italy, Spain and France while avoiding the very worst in Bangladesh and India
- Open a new division producing vegan leather clothing, shoes and handbags

Before going further, our senior executive goes to Cousin Phil (the president of the company's leading brand).

Cousin Phil is adamant: Are you crazy? I have been in this business 25 years and I can tell you that our consumers don't give a damn about pollution. They care only about design and status. If you open this can of worms, you will put us all out of business!

> And Cousin Phil is right. At least until the moment he is wrong at which point the whole company folds and Cousin Phil goes on to write his best-selling book *Adventures in the Skin Trade*.

What is true of the customer side is equally true for the supplier side.

> Case Study II: From Product Maker to Service Supplier – or Not
>
> A factory owner operating in a cheap labor country believes that he should start moving from the role of simple product maker to more sophisticated service provider. This will require some worker training as well as better educated technicians and managers, but he believes the services will more than pay for themselves. Before going further, our factory goes to Cousin Phil (the head of the national industry organization).
>
> Cousin Phil is adamant: Are you crazy? I have been in this business 25 years and I can tell you that our customers don't give a damn about services. They care only about low FOB price. Take my advice. Concentrate on keeping wage rates down, overtime up and number of days off at a minimum. That is what built our industry in the past and will keep us going in the future.
>
> And Cousin Phil is right. It is what we call a self-fulfilling prophecy. Customers come to this country for cheap basic zero-service goods. Both the customer and supplier sides agree – come here for basic goods. If you want fashion goods with services, go elsewhere.
>
> The problem, however, is that local factories as well as concerned outsiders get upset when customers keep fighting for lower and ever lower CM prices. But since low CM price is the only thing these factories offer, it is hardly surprising that customer/factory negotiations would be focused entirely on the subject of CM price.

Despite the many changes that have occurred through the years, senior managers in our industry still prefer the time-honored LET'S-ASK-COUSIN-PHIL system. There are two reasons:

- Managers do not have to make the decisions.
- In the event the decision does not lead to the expected result, management can argue it's not their fault. They went to the best for advice.

Survival in the future requires a very different scenario. Here managers make the decisions that they are being paid to make. But this scenario will require a new set of tools. And in a world where everything will be measured in terms of profit and loss, decisions must all be based on costs relative to benefit. Hence the need for a book about costings.

There are many books on garment costing. This one is different simply because most of what we know about costing is incomplete, incorrect and wrong. To begin with, we are taught that a factory garment costing is a list of costs, usually material, trim and CM (labor + factory overhead + factory profit), which together add up to FOB cost. The problem is that neither the factory FOB costing nor FOB itself is relevant.

As every factory owner knows, the fact that the factory FOB cost totals $10 does not mean the customer will pay $10 because the customer does not care about the factory's cost. He cares only about price and price is determined by value. If the customer thinks the product is worth $10, either because it is the cheapest in the market, or because the factory is offering something of value, he will pay the $10. If, on the other hand, he does not see the value, he will not pay the $10. I am not saying anything that factory owners everywhere do not already know.

Let's face it, in today's world of garment sourcing, where the customer has already gone to the mill and negotiated the price of the fabric and where he has designated every trim supplier and price, all that is left to talk about is CM. And, the truth is that if all the factory can provide is CM, it is already halfway out of business. Again, I am not saying anything that everyone does not already know.

However, what might be new is that if the factory can provide the customer with value in excess of $10, it can charge even more than $10. To take this a step further, to make money the factory has to first find out what their customers want; how much it will cost to give them what they want; and how much they will pay to get what they want.

This is the difference between factories that are fighting every day to keep their heads above water, and the other factories, big and small, who understand the secret and who are already cashing in.

This is a standalone work: a manual for what I have been calling, for those of you familiar with my work over the past 15 years or so, Full Value Costing. Its purpose is to show you how to quantify both costs and value and, in doing so, increase both the factory's profit while at the same time the customer's profits.

The good news is that to move up to Full Value Costing, you do not need a Harvard or Oxford MBA or a PhD in IT/Mathematics. Furthermore the data a factory needs is already compiled by their operation. If I have done my job correctly, by the time you have finished reading this book, if you are a factory owner, you will be able to provide your customer with services of ever-increasing value earning ever-increasing profits for both sides. And if you are a customer, you will have a better understanding of how the suppliers you are working with can become tomorrow's more profitable suppliers and bring you quantifiable benefits at the same time.

There is another purpose to this book. We operate in a constantly changing industry, where today's winners are very often tomorrow's losers and where tomorrow's winners might not even exist today. This book will also provide you with very important information about where the industry is going and where you should be going if you want to be at the cutting edge.

The book will discuss the different types of customer/supplier relationships. Since the inception of the modern global garment industry in the early 1950s, the industry has operated within three strategic models:

>   a. Competitive Model
>   In the early days, when products were limited to cheap basic commodities such as t-shirts, cotton casual pants, basic woven shirts and underwear, customers' expectations were perforce extremely low: A DECENT GARMENT SHIPPED ON TIME AT A LOW, LOW PRICE. Very quickly, supplier selection became a zero-sum game where the lowest FOB price won the order. Because there were many more factories than customers, factories became disposable tools – if low prices forced one factory to go out of business, there were two more ready to take its place.
>
>   In turn, the factory took the same position with regard to its workers. Because workers were for the most part semi-skilled semi-literate women, they too were seen as disposable tools. If 10 workers quit, there were 20 more ready to take their places. This was the era of the zero-service factory where suppliers were equipped to do nothing more than cut & sew. Today, nearly seven decades later, despite sophisticated modern technology, many customers still remain firmly trapped in the competitive strategy mentality. The competitive model is particularly prevalent in South Asia, Cambodia and the Caribbean countries.
>
>   b. Cooperative Model
>   In the mid-1970s, the move from commodity to fashion created an opportunity for change on both the customer and the supplier side. Customers (retailers and brands) began to recognize that while pushing down factory manufacturing prices might bring price reductions of 50¢-70¢ per unit, transferring product development work to the factory and developing fast turn could save up to ten times that amount. Where once factories were limited to the status of product makers, they could now be upgraded to become service suppliers.
>
>   The customer and supplier recognized that to meet the needs of the industry, they had to cooperate with each other to develop the necessary services. Under this new cooperative model strategy, the zero-sum competitive model slowly began to go out of fashion reduced to a large degree to factories producing only commodities or subcontractors. At the top of the cooperative model pyramid were the full-service transnational giants and the specialist factories able to achieve strategic-supplier status.

c. Collaborative Model
This model is still in a nascent state. The new industry customers, particularly both large and smaller e-commerce companies, are the catalyst for this latest model. Under this new model, the entire supply chain is hollowed out. In the cooperative model, the customer gave the supplier increased responsibilities. In the collaborative model, the role of the customers is reduced to the first stages – determining what the consumer wants and providing the factory with the original design – and the final sales and marketing stage. Everything else is ceded to the factory.

In this new model, both the customer and supplier side recognize that neither side can move forward without the other. Consequently the relationship between the customer and supplier is a true partnership. Where originally this concept was limited to the newcomer customers, we now see a growing realization that what is relevant to e-commerce people is equally relevant to the industry as a whole.

This book also talks about making money. We are all in business to make money. The more profitable strategy should be the strategy of choice. In order to determine real profits, we need real costings. The costings of the oldest competitive model have for the most part been superseded although they are still employed by some of the leading brands and retailers.

Customers who have adopted the cooperative model recognize that important costs come from areas where the zero-service factory cannot play a role. By cooperating with a full-service factory, the customer can markedly reduce their costs even after paying the full-service factory a premium for their value-added services.

As the customer increasingly benefits from the suppliers' services, their demands for value-added services increase to the point where almost all preproduction, all production and most postproduction is given over to the supplier. This is the collaborative model.

These three models reflect the changing customer/supplier relationship from the competitive, where the supplier is seen as a disposable tool, to the cooperative, where the supplier is seen as an important asset, to the collective where customer and supplier join together in partnership.

Evolution seldom takes place uniformly across the board. The global garment industry follows the same pattern: some remain trapped in an already outmoded competitive system. Others, having moved ahead to the more efficient cooperative system, will in turn become trapped when the industry moves on, making the previous seemingly more efficient system in turn outmoded. Finally, there are those who recognize that the future lies with the collaborative system where customer and supplier become locked together to create greater value and increased profits for both sides.

BOOK I
Tools of the Trade

Chapter 1
Tools

Question: What does a cost sheet have in common with a screwdriver or an MBA degree?

Clues: Nobody buys a screwdriver because it is aesthetically pleasing. Its sole purpose is to turn screws clockwise or counterclockwise. Likewise, a person may spend a lifetime as an amateur studying mannerist art, the battle of Lützen, or understanding G-d, and at the end consider his or her life well spent, but despite what some may write on a graduate school application, no one actually wants to spend their life trying to understand capital depreciation.

Answer: Garment cost sheets, MBA degrees and screwdrivers are all tools. The value of a tool is solely the degree to which it works, which is why no one would choose to buy a paper screwdriver, an MBA degree from Trump University or a cost sheet that does not work.

The purpose of this book is to create the best working cost sheet. The following is a basic cost sheet, familiar to all factory professionals. We will use this basic cost sheet throughout the book. (For our purposes it is sufficient to note that Net Profit is calculated at 5% of total FOB price; CM is calculated at 30% of FOB price; CM Labor is based on about 60% sewing and the rest for ancillary labor and calculated for a worker earning $150/26-day month and working ten hours per day; CM Overhead is calculated at an industry average of 2.9 times labor cost.)

Basic Cost Sheet		
Material	60%	$6.00
Trim	10%	$1.00
CM	30%	$3.00
FOB	100%	$10.00

CM Breakdown	
Labor	$0.64
Net Profit	$0.50
Overhead	$1.86

Traditionally cost sheets serve two purposes:

1. Externally: To negotiate FOB prices with the customers. However, as discussed in the preface, customers no longer negotiate price on the basis of factory cost, but rather on the value the factory can provide.

2. Internally: To provide information for factory management to make the best decisions. It is in this area that the basic cost sheet provides its greatest value. The good news is that every factory already has the information required for materials and trims:

The Guide to Cost-to-Value Analysis

    a. Fabric to be supplied
        i. Name of the fabric supplier
        ii. Cost per meter of the fabric
        iii. Fabric consumption per piece

    b. Description of each required trim item
        i. Name of specific trim supplier
        ii. Cost per unit of each trim item
        iii. Quantity required of each trim item

With this information, the factory can move from manual to computerized purchasing of all fabric and trim. This provides multiple benefits: greater efficiency, reduced time and cost, fewer errors and most important, greater security. At the same time, computerized purchasing of material and trim is necessary in order to carry out the next step which is calculating the job costing.

Job Costing

The cost sheet is the factory's list of estimated materials and processes. The purpose of the job costing is to determine the actual cost of the order and how that total cost differs from the estimated costs shown on the cost sheet, which can be determined only after all the orders produced during the period have been shipped. The job costing is the actual costs of the order and comprised of:

Total Materials:
    a. Total cost of fabric
    b. Total cost of trim

Total CM:
    c. Total wages
    d. Total overhead
    e. Total net profit

In real life, however, there are difficulties with each of the items listed above. Let's look first at the fabric where there are two interrelated problems. How does a factory account for leftover fabric? 50,000 meters were delivered and after cutting all orders for that fabric, there are 600 mts left. The factory initially has two choices:

- Add the leftover fabric to the fabric costs of the various styles on a pro rata basis;
- Add the additional fabric to inventory thus listing the fabric as an asset.

But then you have to look at the fabric type. If the fabric is 125g white jersey and the factory's business is t-shirts, of course the leftover fabric can be added to inventory. But if the fabric is chartreuse rayon shirting with puce polka dots which no future customer is likely to want, the factory has no choice but to add a pro rata cost to each unit produced.

The second issue is how to prorate the added cost of fabric among the styles that used the same fabric. This is what is known as the joint-cost problem. There are again two choices:

- Apportion the cost of the fabric on the basis of consumption;
- Apportion the cost of the fabric on the basis of FOB price

Trim costing is more straightforward. While joint-cost problems involving fabric are relatively unusual, those involving trim are extremely common and complicated. With the possible exception of customer's labels, the cost of all purchased trim should be applied to the order. The leftover trim is not included in inventory for accounting purposes, but it does exist and might be usable for future orders.

Labor Costing Calculations

The factory's records will show how many sewers worked on the style, the number of days the sewers spent on the style, and the total wages received. To this must be added the ancillary labor data – cutting, bundling, QC, pressing, packing, etc. The factory's account department has records of total wages for the designated period. If, for example, wages for the period totaled $1000 of which sewers received $667, then for the purpose of wage calculations, ancillary wages may be estimated to equal 50% of sewing wages. One year is the period on which to base the calculations to average out seasonal fluctuations in the annual data.

Overhead Costing Calculations

There are two problems here. The first involves how overhead is broken down. The factory's account department can provide data for total overhead for the period. The problem is how to break down total overhead to overhead-per-unit. The simplest and most practical solution is to relate overhead cost to labor. We know that the more difficult styles take longer than the easy styles and therefore the overhead should be greater. Labor cost per unit also reflects the degree of difficulty. Therefore we can calculate overhead as a proportion of labor.

The second problem relates to seasonality. A factory is a closed-room operation where there is a maximum level of production. Sometimes production reaches 100% of capacity. But because our industry operates on a seasonal basis, there are months when production falls below capacity. Therefore, the annual average must be less than 100% of capacity and we cannot base overhead on 100% capacity. Working with the account department, the factory can come up with a reasonable estimate for overall annual capacity. A reasonable overall annual figure might be 70%, a figure that we will be using for our subsequent calculations.

The Guide to Cost-to-Value Analysis

Here is what monthly exports over a year might look like:

Percentage Garment Exports by Month													
Month	01	02	03	04	05	06	07	08	09	10	11	12	
% of Annual	8.6%	7.3%	5.2%	5.8%	6.6%	8.4%	10.8%	11.8%	11.1%	10.2%	7.3%	6.9%	
Value ($.000)	859	735	522	582	656	836	1081	1179	1113	1021	729	687	1000

In a world without seasons, the volume of business would remain constant each month at 8.33%, because 8.33% times 12 months equals 99.99%. In the chart above, exports in March were less than half of exports in August, meaning overheads per unit in March were more than double that in August.

Net Profit is what remains after accounting for all costs.

One of the most important purposes of the job costing is to determine where real costs deviate from the cost sheet so that factory management can overcome similar errors in the future. In the case study below, the greatest loss came from increased overhead. While there are a number of factors that may account for deviations in overhead costs, the most common factor is seasonality, particularly when the rise (or fall) is substantial. Total overhead is by definition fixed. Therefore, overhead per unit rises in low season and falls in high season.

Work in Process

At the end of any period, there are orders that are still undergoing processing. While we do not want to distort the job-costing process, a method of allocation between the current period and the next period is required. Any decision will be to a large degree arbitrary but it must be based on readily available data. I suggest that all the pieces that have completed sewing by the end of the period be allocated. All pieces that have not completed the sewing process should be held over to the following period.

Job Costings as Management Tool

The job costing is a very important management tool. It provides important information not available elsewhere. Let's look at this example where basic and job costing figures are compared.

Chapter 1 Tools

Case Study III: Basic Costing vs Job Costing

The factory has an order for 10,000 pieces.

Basic Costing: 10,000 pieces

Material	60%	$60,000			
Trim	10%	$10,000			
CM	30%	$30,000	CM Breakdown		
FOB	100%	$100,000	Labor	$6,410.26	
			Overhead	$18,589.74	2.9
Total Cost		$95,000			
Total Revenue		$100,000			
Net Profit	5.00%	$5,000			

However, the actual job costing turns out to tell a very different story.

Job Costing: 10,000 pieces

Material	60%	$61,000			
Trim	10%	$9,300			
			Labor	$6,169.88	
			Overhead	$22,307.69	4
Total Cost		$98,778			
Total Revenue		$99,300			
Net Profit	0.53%	$522			

What happened?

Material: The factory ordered 30,000 meters of our well-known chartreuse shirting with puce polka dots, but received 30,500 meters. Rather than cutting the additional fabric (which under the normal contract allowing for 3% overshipment they were entitled to do), the outstanding 500 meters was written off but the extra $1000 cost still had to be added.

Trim: The factory enjoyed a 7% savings because the cost of the trim taken from stock was greater than the cost of the trim overage which was also written off.

Labor: Here again the factory did well. The costing listed production time at 40 SAM (standard allowed minutes), but the actual production time was 38.5 SAM.

Overhead: This was where the factory incurred the big loss. The basic costing was based on $1.86 per unit (2.9 times labor) but due to the fact that the order was produced during a slow period when total orders were less than capacity, the overhead in fact increased from $1.86 per unit to $2.23 per unit (4 times labor).

Total Revenue: 10000 pieces cut but only 9930 shipped with the result that total revenue was reduced from $100,000 to $99,300.

Net Profit: Drops from a theoretical $5000 (5% of FOB) for the order to only $522 (0.52% of FOB).

The Guide to Cost-to-Value Analysis

An accurate job costing sheet allows the factory to determine which customer provides the greatest profit:

Net Profit by Customer by Period			
Customer Name	Total Sales	Gross Profit	Net Profit
Able	$1000	12.5%	4.0%
Baker	$800	30.0%	12.0%
Charlie	$700	20.0%	6.0%
Delta	$550	5.0%	-3.0%
Echo	$400	16.0%	1.0%
Frank	$320	16.0%	2.0%

Similarly, the factory can determine which product is the most profitable:

Product: Circular Knit (cut & sew)			
Product	Total sales	Gross Profit	Net Profit
T-shirt	$1000	10.0%	2.5%
Polo shirt	$700	15.0%	4.5%
Fashion blouse	$500	30.0%	8.0%
Dress	$550	40.0%	15.0%

Branch Factories

Factory groups with multiple branch operations should treat each branch as an independent unit. In this way management can compare the performance of one branch over another. There are important factors to consider:

- The branch factory should not be subsidized for work performed by the head factory. For example, if the head factory provides product development, the added cost of product development should be added to the branch factory cost sheet.
- The branch factory that performs special services should benefit from those services. For example, if the branch offers fast turn, both the added cost and profit should be included in the branch factory cost sheet.
- If the branch factory offers value to the customer completely apart from anything it does, such as close proximity or duty-free access, those benefits should also be included in the cost sheet.

Subcontractors

For the purpose of costings, the relationship between the factory and the subcontractor should be the same as an agent with the factory, with the subcontractor playing the role of a separate factory. As with any agent-factory relationship, gross profit should be calculated as a commission.

Chapter 1 Tools

Once again, the factory does not want to subsidize the work of the subcontractor. It is therefore important that all work provided by the parent company be part of the overhead to be deducted from the gross profit.

As the industry progresses, and the role of the supplier becomes increasingly more important, qualified factories no longer have to accept any order, from any customer, at any price. In this new model industry, the factory will have the choice of which customer it wants to work with.

The data obtained from the job costing is an indispensable tool allowing the factory to make the right choices, whether they are choosing one customer over another or one product over another. Customers and products for orders during low season will also be highly valued.

Chapter 2
Static v Dynamic Cost Sheets

As discussed in the previous chapter, the basic cost sheet relates only to FOB cost.

Basic Cost Sheet		
Fabric	60%	$6.00
Trim	10%	$1.00
CM	30%	$3.00
FOB	100%	$10.00

The problem is that the basic cost sheet, while undoubtedly accurate as far as it goes, does not go far enough. For example, the cost sheet shows fabric cost to be $6.00 (2mts @ $3.00/mt). If the price of fabric rose to $3.50/mt, then the fabric cost would rise by 16%, increasing the FOB price from $10 to $11, an increase of 10%.

In fact a 10% increase in FOB price may not necessarily cause an increase in the customer's cost. For example, if a factory located in Mexico replaced the made-in-China fabric with fabric produced locally, or in Canada or the U.S, its products would be entitled to duty-free access to the U.S. The cost of fabric may have increased from $6.00 to $7.00, but the savings on duty, $1.62, would have more than compensated for the $1.00 increased FOB cost for the fabric.

	Chinese Fabric vs Local Fabric				
	Chinese Fabric			Local Fabric	
	% of Total LDP Cost	Cost	Cost		% of Total LDP Cost
Fabric	60.0%	$6.00	$7.00		63.6%
Trim	10.0%	$1.00	$1.00		9.1%
CM	30.0%	$3.00	$3.00		27.3%
FOB	100.0%	$10.00	$11.00		100.0%
Duty	16.2%	$1.62	$0.00		
LDP*		$11.62	$11.00		

*Landed Duty Paid

The problem is that the basic cost sheet is static, complete in itself, but unable to take into consideration any outside factors. As we will see, the value of every single cost factor is based on other cost factors. If we do not include these other cost factors, we have no way to determine actual costs. When I write every cost factor, I do mean every cost factor.

The Guide to Cost-to-Value Analysis

For example, which is more expensive: air freight or sea freight? Taken by itself we would all have to agree that air freight is far more costly than sea freight. However, if we look further, we might also have to agree that in many cases 10-hour freight time compared to 10-day freight time may well be worth the additional cost. Unfortunately, in our basic cost sheet, there is no way to include the relative value of air vs sea freight.

When we criticize a cost sheet, it is usually because the numbers are wrong. The button did not cost $6.00/gross. The garment did not require 24 minutes production time. The overhead per unit was not $1.74. In addition, these errors are almost always incremental. The button cost was $7.00/gross. The production time was 28 minutes. The overhead per unit was $2.54. Really serious problems occur because we failed to include other cost factors. In the case shown above, the exclusion of import duty in the basic cost sheet resulted in an error of $1.62, an amount greater than the trim cost, the total CM labor cost, and almost equal to the total CM overhead cost.

The effects of the failure to include all costs have been aggravated as customer strategies evolved over time. In the early days the customer engaged in GARMENT BUYING whereby the factory supplied all materials and manufacturing and made added profit on both materials and CM. Later customers moved to GARMENT SOURCING, whereby the customer negotiated prices for all materials directly with the fabric mill and all trim suppliers, leaving only CM prices open for negotiation.

Recently more sophisticated buyers have moved to OPEN SOURCING whereby new technology has given them the ability to calculate all cost factors including material consumption and, more importantly, the number of minutes required to produce the garment. In this case, the only area open for negotiation is the cost per minute. Under open sourcing, the customer no longer negotiates prices on a per style basis but rather on all styles to be produced during a specific period entirely on a cost-per-minute basis. For example, if the customer pays 6¢ per minute, he will pay CM $1.20 for all garments requiring 20 minutes production time regardless of the style.

As the industry moves from garment buying to garment sourcing to open sourcing, those factories still trapped in the old system will eventually be forced out of business because they cannot see beyond the static world of fabric, trim and CM. Those who understand the dynamics of cost and who include all cost factors in their cost sheet will see the move to garment sourcing and open sourcing as an opportunity, an opening door that will increase their profit. If anything, as customers increasingly depend on open sourcing, smart factories will be in the driver's seat with customers only too happy to accept their conditions.

For the factory, the purpose of the cost sheet is therefore not only to show you how to define costs, it is to show you how to create value. Factories still operating under the old system know that in a world where the customer already knows the cost of fabric and trim, if they can only offer ever lower CMs, they cannot survive.

To survive the factory has to provide increased value not just to the customer but to its own bottom line as well.

Chapter 3
Intrinsic Cost Savings

Every effort on the part of management to increase profit by reducing costs can be divided into two parts:

- Added Cost: the investment of time, effort, and capital
- Added Value: the profit derived from the investment

When the cost of the investment is paid for by the company and the value received goes back to the same company, we define this as **INTRINSIC COST SAVINGS.**

These cost savings can be based on work by either the customer or by the supplier side but as intrinsic costs, these cost savings are not related to the other side. Work carried out by the factory benefits only the factory where work carried out by the brand or retailer customer benefits only that customer.

Contrast this to extrinsic cost savings which will be covered in Chapter 5 where work carried out by one side benefits the other side. Examples include the factory carrying out product development work for the benefit of the customer or the customer sending engineers to the factory to improve their scheduling capacity calculations.

The Customer Side

Cost savings may come from different areas:

- Expansion to new markets
- Added products
- Introduction of new technology
- Garment cost reduction

The Factory Side

Cost savings may come from different areas. The two involving increased productivity are most relevant to our work:

- Capital investment in high-tech equipment
- Capital investment in worker training

Investment in high-tech machinery to increase productivity

Assume a machine that costs $25,000 will do the work of four sewers. This sounds pretty good. With enough investment, a factory with 200 sewers could be reduced to 50 sewers. But let's look closer at the numbers.

The Guide to Cost-to-Value Analysis

Let's assume the following:
1. Cost of the machine will be amortized over a period of 5 years = $5000 per year
2. Interest at 5% = $625 per year
3. Cost = $5,625 per year
4. Cost per month = $468.75

Investment in Capital Equipment Replaces 4 Workers @ $150/month Wage					
Machine cost	Annual Amortization	Interest	Cost Per Annum	Cost Per Month
	5 yrs	5.0%		$12.00
$25,000.00	$5,000.00	$625.00	$5,625.00	$468.75

To calculate the capital cost per minute, we divide the total number of working minutes per month (10hrs/day x 26 days/mo = 15600 minutes). This comes to 3cts/minute. The capital cost of a 40-minute garment is therefore $1.20.

Capital Cost per Unit (40 min/pc)		
Per Month	Per Minute	Per Unit
$468.75	$0.03	$1.20

The table below shows that how the investment of one machine that replaces four workers breaks even on a per-unit basis.

For the cost sheet, we now use material and trim costs multiplied by four since we are talking about the work done by four workers. Capital investment stays at $1.20 because there is only one machine.

We then have to calculate the sewing labor cost per unit. Here we go back to the 15600minutes/worker/month divided by the $150/mo wage. That works out to 0.96cts/minute or 38cts per 40-minute garment.

Sewing labor only represents part of the CM total labor, about 60%. The rest is made up of labor from other departments (cutting, pressing, packing etc.) which is not affected by capital investment calculations. CM Overhead remains the same because the number of units produced is unchanged, only the number of workers decreases.

Chapter 3   Intrinsic Cost Savings

	Capital Investment of 1 Machine Replaces 4 Workers			
	No Capital Investment		After Capital Investment	
	Cost Factor	Cost	Cost	Cost Factor
Material	60%	$24.00	$24.00	
Trim	10%	$4.00	$4.00	
Capital Investment		$0.00	$1.20	
CM Labor Sewing		$1.54	$0.38	
CM Labor Other		$0.77	$0.77	
CM Overhead*		$6.69	$6.69	
FOB		$37.00	$37.04	-$0.04

*CM Overhead calculated at industry average of 2.9x total CM Labor

But there are other issues to consider. How many factories in developing countries have access to funds for capital investment? To make matters worse, we haven't even factored in yet the cost of maintenance. Furthermore, the 50 remaining workers would not be illiterate semi-skilled sewers but rather university graduates with engineering degrees. And if we are located in South or Southeast Asia, we have to ask if we can find qualified engineers in our area, and if so, how much would we have to pay them.

There is a good reason why the new technology is successful only in factories located in industrialized countries. Imagine you are H.B. Schlogvessel, a factory owner in an industrialized country. You are faced with the same problem. Wages are indeed rising. Unlike your counterpart located in a developing country who can no longer afford to pay his workers $150 a month for a 60+ hour week, you are paying $3000 a month for an eight-hour day, five days a week. You are in an altogether different position. In your case the machine is cheaper than the worker. Your investment practically pays off even if the $25,000 capital investment replaces one worker and you get real savings if it replaces two workers.

	Capital Investment 1 Machine Replaces 2 Workers			
	No Capital Investment		After Capital Investment	
	Cost Factor	Cost	Cost	Cost Factor
Material	60%	$12.00	$12.00	
Trim	10%	$4.00	$4.00	
Capital Investment		$0.00	$1.20	
CM Labor Sewing		$17.79	$8.89	
CM Labor Other		$8.89	$8.89	
CM Overhead		$26.68	$26.68	
FOB		$69.37	$61.66	Factory Savings $7.70

The Guide to Cost-to-Value Analysis

From these calculations, it is obvious that only manufacturers in the industrialized countries will benefit from the current high-tech revolution. But there are exceptions. For example, for a few products such as sweaters and hosiery, computerized machinery can reduce the number of workers to the point where capital investment could be amortized profitably even in the least developed countries (LDC). Similarly, manufacturers in middle-income countries can invest profitably in some high-tech machinery such as computerized laser cutting and computerized garment sorting to provide pick & pack distribution and delivery services.

Investment in Worker Training to Increase Productivity

There is a vast difference between productivity in industrialized countries and the garment-exporting countries located in the developing and least developed country world. In industrialized countries, a 2%-3% increase in productivity is considered to be very good news. But in many garment-exporting countries, productivity remains very low and increases can be quite high. A garment which requires 40 minutes in most countries can be produced in 20 minutes in China. We have seen productivity increases of 25% are possible in low-productivity countries in a few short months provided the factory has access to world-class engineers and is willing to make the investment.

In industrialized countries, where labor rates are high and overhead relatively low, the benefit of higher productivity is reduced labor cost. In most garment-producing countries, where labor rates are very low and overheads relatively high, the greatest benefit of increased productivity is reduced overhead.

For the purpose of our calculations, we will assume the following:

- a. Labor cost = 64¢ per garment (40 minutes @ 1.6¢ per minute)
- b. Productivity at 50% = 40 minutes per garment
- c. Pieces per machine per day before productivity increase = 15 (600mins/day ÷ 40 minutes per garment)
- d. After 25% increased productivity = 32 minutes per garment and 18.75pcs per machine per day
- e. Cost of training = $250,000 or $2,083.33/month (amortized over 12 months)
- f. A 250-machine factory at 30 minutes per garment has a capacity of 130,000 units per month (250 machines x 26 days x 20 units/machine/day)
- g. Estimating average production at 75% capacity, the factory will produce 97,500 units per month
- h. Cost of training per unit ($2083 ÷ 97500) = 21¢

Based on a cost of $250,000 for the training, the garment cost rises by 21¢ per unit. At the same time, labor cost falls now by 20% per unit or 13¢. More importantly the overhead per unit also falls by 20% = 61¢ total overhead savings.

Chapter 3 Intrinsic Cost Savings

Furthermore, once the training has been completed, the cost of update training in subsequent years falls considerably.

25% Increased Productivity from 40 to 30 minutes per garment				
	No Worker Training		After Worker Training	
	Factor	Cost	Cost	Factor
Material	60%	$6.00	$6.00	
Trim	10%	$1.00	$1.00	
CM Labor		$0.64	$0.48	75%
CM Overhead		$1.86	$1.40	75%
CM Total Cost		$2.50	$1.88	
Added Training Cost		$0.00	$0.21	
Total Cost		$9.50	$9.09	
Total Revenue		$10.00	$10.00	
Net Profit	5%	$0.50	$0.91	9.1%

There is yet another advantage to using worker training to increase productivity. In a world where there is constant pressure for higher wages, factory management may decide to return the 16cts of cost savings to the workers effectively increasing wages by 33%. The factory's profit would be reduced to 75cts which still represents 7.5% of FOB or 50% higher than their old 5% profit.

But advanced worker training can present its own difficulties. Increasing worker productivity depends not just on developing new skill sets, but more importantly on worker empowerment. Henry Ford, the inventor of the old fashion assembly line factory, is known to have lamented, "Why is it every time I ask for a pair of hands, they come with a brain attached? New methods of training and production require more than workers' hands. The worker now becomes the factory's greatest capital asset and it is precisely for this reason that investments are being made.

We recognize that cost sheets must provide both comprehensive and accurate information. There is yet another equally important consideration. Full value cost sheets may involve literally thousands of mathematical relationships and millions of pieces of data. This is easy for the computer but most people need everything boiled down to a one-page report that answers a specific question in a readily understandable manner.

So ideally when the guy comes to sell you a robotic piece of machinery, as factory owner, you should be able to go to your AI computer with a simple request:

The Guide to Cost-to-Value Analysis

> You: Irving, THIS GUY WANTS TO SELL ME A MACHINE FOR $250,000 WHICH WILL TAKE THE PLACE OF FOUR WORKERS. SHOULD I BUY?
>
> Irving the AI Computer: ARE YOU OUT OF YOUR MIND? FOUR GETS YOU NOWHERE. THE MACHINE WOULD HAVE TO REPLACE MORE THAN 10 WORKERS JUST TO BREAK EVEN.

EU and China

The importance of intrinsic cost reduction cannot be overemphasized. The most important examples to look at here are Greater China (includes Hong Kong) and the EU. We think of them as two very different entities, yet they share many points in common, the most important of which is that they are both home to very successful export-garment industries.

As we can see from the chart below, as of 2019, together they accounted for 49% of total global garment exports:

\multicolumn{4}{c}{World's Top 10 Garment Exporters 2019}			
Rank	Country	Value $mn	Market Share
1	EU	134,531	28.6%
2	G. China	97,465	20.7%
3	Bangladesh	40,715	8.7%
4	Vietnam	30,038	6.4%
5	India	16,508	3.5%
6	Turkey	15,540	3.3%
7	Indonesia	8,246	1.8%
8	Cambodia	8,287	1.8%
9	Pakistan	5,843	1.2%
10	Sri Lanka	5,638	1.2%

Source ITC Geneva

There are many reasons why together Greater China and the EU dominate the global export-garment industry. China and the EU have much in common:

- easy access to locally produced materials
- ease of doing business
- concentration on sophisticated fashion products
- educated management, technical specialists and well-trained workers
- strong domestic demand particularly for fashion clothing

Chapter 3 Intrinsic Cost Savings

But there are also differences between the two, the most important of which is FOB price. As we can see from the chart below, EU FOB prices are substantially higher than FOB prices from China for the same product.

FOB Price Comparison EU vs Greater China (in year of latest data)				
HTS	Description	FOB EU	FOB China	Year
6205.20	Men's cotton woven shirts	$15.11	$5.99	2015
6203.31	Men's wool jacket	$111.31	$47.27	2019
6203.41	Men's wool pants	$40.94	$26.11	2019
6203.42	Men's cotton pants	$16.41	$6.51	2016
6204.42	Women's dresses	$21.93	$6.60	2016
6204.61	Women's wool pants	$51.39	$21.62	2019
6204.62	Women's cotton pants	$14.29	$6.04	2018
6209.10	Cotton t-shirts	$4.18	$2.99	2015
6110.11	Wool sweaters	$41.37	$14.75	2019
6110.20	Cotton sweaters	$11.86	$6.68	2015

Source: ITC

This difference results from two important advantages for the EU which allows EU brands and the factories that produce for them to charge more for their products:

1. Design Strength: The EU is home to the world's greatest agglomeration of design centers including Italy, France, Spain, Netherlands, Sweden, Germany, etc. Importers placing orders in the EU generally rely on EU design. Contrast this with China where the customers placing orders provide their own designs, often of EU origin.

2. Brand Cachet: Made-in-Italy, Made-in-France, Made-in-Spain etc. brings a cachet which allows the importing retailer and/or brand to charge a higher price. Some may claim that this brand cachet is unwarranted, but we have to accept that these EU-based brands create value which Made-in-China lacks.

All of which, brings us back to the underlying basis of this book:

Price is based on value. The greater value offered by EU-based suppliers once again has been translated into higher price.

Finally, this analysis explains why the EU has a vibrant and successful garment industry, while the U.S. industry cannot compete in the international market.

The Guide to Cost-to-Value Analysis

1. Design: The U.S. has more than its fair share of talented designers (many of whom work for European companies). But designers working for U.S. companies play a very limited role in the design process. Most U.S. retailers and brands care about FOB price above design, with the result that the design work must be dumbed down to meet the skill limitations of the factories that they choose to work with. At the same time, in an effort to increase market share, management also dumbs down the design because edgy will often not sell, while lowest-common-denominator is risk-free. The result is very low design integrity: The sample does not resemble the sketch and the stock does not resemble the sample.

2. Brand: Made-in-the-USA is a political statement, not a fashion statement, which is why foreign retailers and brands do well in the U.S., while the U.S. seldom does well in the rest of the world.

Chapter 4
Intrinsic Costs: Schedules and Capacity

The well-run factory depends on detailed real-time information of two interrelated factors:

- Schedules
- Capacity

Schedules

From the very first step, long before production begins or any materials are ordered, the factory must create a schedule. The schedule starts at the end with the final date: STOCK GARMENTS PACKED. To reach this point we have perhaps seven major events, each of which must occur on or before a specific date if the order is to be shipped on time.

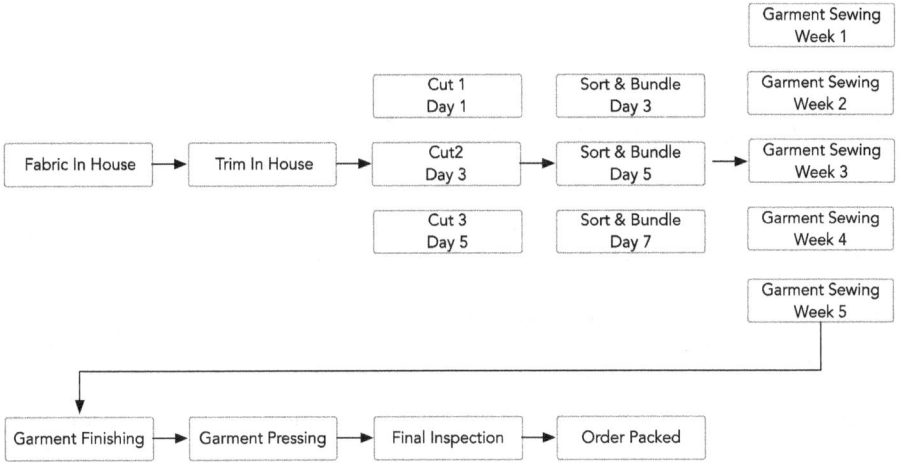

Some of the steps are obvious, or at least should be. To begin the process, you need all the materials – fabrics and trims. Trims require considerable advance planning. A garment may require anywhere between five to 25 trim items. The failure of the zipper to arrive on time is equally as serious as the fabric not arriving on time because in neither case can production start. Therefore the schedule must include the arrival date of each and every single item.

Some steps require special consideration. Probably the most important step in the process is GARMENT SEWING. To arrive at a reasonable cost figure, we have to consider a number of factors such as the difficulty of the style, availability of equipment and the size of the order. We must first determine how many minutes are required to sew one piece. This is often a relatively straightforward calculation: we look for a similar style that has been produced in the past.

The Guide to Cost-to-Value Analysis

Our costing template requires the following:
- Number of sewing lines;
- Number of sewing machines in each line;
- Number of sewing days required to complete order

From this we can easily determine the number of minutes per machine per garment. In the beginning, the estimates will often be less than accurate. However, with time, estimates and reality will coincide.

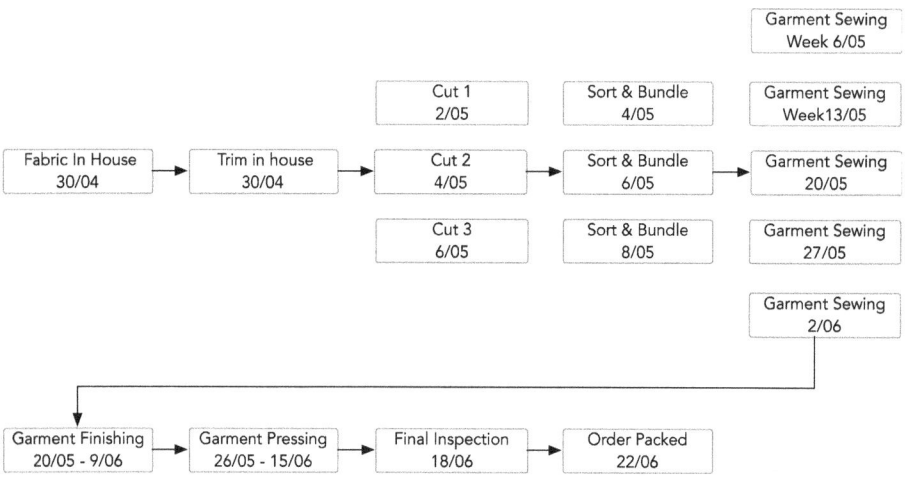

Individually, each schedule not only defines the time required to complete each order, but more importantly, determines the moment that delays and/or problems occur that will affect the final delivery date. While the prudent factory will include extra time in each schedule to allow for unforeseen delays and problems, that extra time may still prove insufficient. For example, if the zippers arrive one week late, on 7 May, the completion date of 22 June may well be delayed until 29 June. The customer should be notified of expected delays as soon as possible. They won't be happy but knowing 30 days in advance about a delayed shipment is much more preferable to finding out at the last minute.

Furthermore, when compiling schedules, overtime production has its own considerations. Factory professionals recognize that time lost is never recovered. Also excessive overtime, while resulting in more production today, gives less production tomorrow – the workers are tired.

Capacity

Collectively, the aggregate of all schedules provides data necessary to measure capacity. Each additional schedule notifies management just how much more business the factory can accept for each period. Overbooking business is regrettably common in our industry, with the result that factories and in some cases entire national industries are branded unreliable.

Chapter 4 Intrinsic Costs Schedules and Capacity

Below is an example of what data needs to go into a capacity report.

Case Study IV: Capacity Report

The figures shown below are hypothetical and should not be taken as an accurate description of a real factory. Imagine the following:

Factory Size:	200 machines
Wages:	$250 per month
Working Days:	26 days per month
Working Hrs:	10 per day
Wages:	1.6¢ per minute

	Wages/month	Days	Hours	Minutes
Amount	$250.00	26	10	60
		$9.62	$0.96	$0.016

Number of total production minutes per month based on 200 machines:

Units	Machine Numbers	Minutes per Worker	Total Minutes
	200	15,600	3,120,000

The following are the confirmed orders at the time of the report for the target month.

Orders for Target Month

	Units per order	Minutes per Piece	Total Minutes
Style 1	6300	30	189,000
Style 2	9000	26	234,000
Style 3	23200	42	974,400
Style 4	11350	37	419,950
Style 5	11200	33	369,600
Total			2,186,950

Percentage Capacity   70.1%

Note that when sales reach 70% of capacity the overhead for the month has been covered.

The Guide to Cost-to-Value Analysis

Coordination Department

All of the scheduling and capacity data is gathered together in a single document compiled by the COORDINATION DEPARTMENT. This is important to all factories but of fundamental importance to vertically integrated operations.

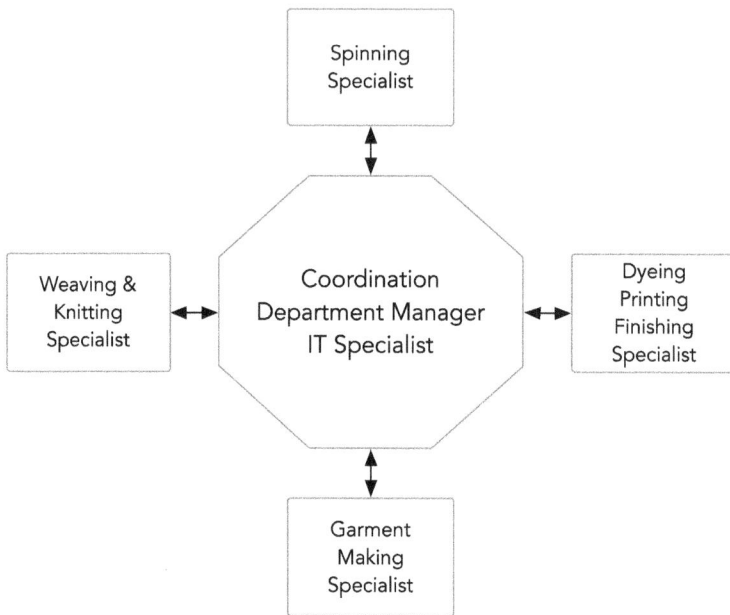

The coordination department plays a key role. While it makes no decisions, it provides the information to management at all levels as well as to customers, who do make the decisions. These are the roles of the coordination department:

1. Post all data related to schedules. Ideally, this information should be available to everyone, including:
   a. Management;
   b. Technical staff dealing with each process; i.e., spinning, weaving or knitting, dyeing-printing-finishing, garment making;
   c. Factory merchandisers dealing with the customer;
   d. Customer who is given a pin number to receive real-time data for their orders.

2. Alert management and all relevant parties to serious problems on a timely basis.

3. Field all communications between factory merchandisers and technical staff in each department.

Coordination in a vertically integrated company is particularly challenging

Chapter 4   Intrinsic Costs Schedules and Capacity

because while sales increase arithmetically, data volume increases exponentially. For a company that is increasing sales at 10% annually, it is not unusual for communications to increase exponentially, 10% in year one, 20% in year two, and 40% in year three.

Some years ago I was retained by a large vertically integrated factory group (circular knitting to dyeing/finishing to garment making) to increase annual sales from $250 million to $500 million. In the 20 months I was there, volume indeed doubled, but the company was forced to completely change their data collection. The single greatest problem was communication. We reached a point where the dye master was receiving 350 internal e-mails a day from merchandisers, technical staff and management. They also received additional emails from outside customers who were ordering fabric for their own factories.

The solution was to create a separate coordination department. Under the new system all queries between the marketing/sales/customer relations and the operation departments would come to the technical specialists in the coordination department who:

a. Provided answers;
b. Met with operation managers to discuss issues and try to work out solutions beneficial to everyone;
c. Kicked some problems up to senior management who decided in the event of unforeseen problems which customers would be given priority and which customers would have to wait.

At the end of the day, the purpose of the coordination department is to ensure there is no interruption in the production flow. Substantial programming work was required to make things work smoothly but the outcome was well worth the effort.

Chapter 5
Extrinsic Cost Savings

As we have already seen, when company management decides on a specific investment project, usually the project can be divided into two parts:

- Added Cost: the investment of time, effort, and capital
- Added Value: the profit derived from the investment

When added cost comes from one company and the added value goes to the other company, we define this as Extrinsic Cost Savings.

These cost savings are based on a cooperative effort between the customer and its factory supplier. Many customers and suppliers do not believe that extrinsic cost savings exist because they believe that cooperation between customer and factory is impossible. Nevertheless the cooperative model does indeed exist and can produce the greatest cost saving.

Here again is our basic cost sheet:

Basic Cost Sheet		
	% Total Cost	Cost
Fabric	60.0%	$6.00
Trim	10.0%	$1.00
CM Labor	6.4%	$0.64
CM Overhead	18.6%	$1.86
CM Total Cost	25.0%	$2.50
Total Cost	95.0%	$9.50
Factory Profit	5.0%	$0.50
Total FOB Cost		$10.00

It is important to note that extrinsic costs cannot be lumped together with overhead. Rather they must remain as separate distinct items in our cost sheet so that we can deal with them apart from other costs.

There are two extremely important extrinsic costs which have never been included in the basic garment cost sheet:

- Product development (sample making, material sourcing, trim selection, etc.)
- Markdowns

The Guide to Cost-to-Value Analysis

Let's look first at the sample making process. At first glance it would appear that sample making is an intrinsic cost for the following reasons:

   a. By definition, the sample must be related to the garment on order;
   b. Production cannot start until a sample is approved;
   c. There must be a quantifiable cost to making a sample.

The reality is different and results from two problems. First of all, most styles that go through the sample making process never go into production. Perhaps two out of every three styles are discarded. To quantify the cost of sample making, we have to include the discards, which are by definition neither related nor required for the garment that goes into production.

Second, we cannot calculate the sample making cost per piece because the cost of the sample making process is unrelated to the size of the final order.

There is a three-step solution to the extrinsic cost problems. They are not 100% accurate, but they are a great deal better than the alternatives. Here are the steps:

1. Quantify the cost of sample making in the supplier country:

   a. Assume a worker is paid $9.62 per day, calculated on the basis of $250 per month for a 26-day month;
   b. Assume overhead equals 290% labor;
   c. Assume that each sample requires 1.5-man days, including sample making, pattern making and other related work;
   d. Assume the following are the requirements for the sample making process:
      i. First sample
      ii. Two duplicates required before designer approves the style
      iii. Two additional styles which never go into production

	Cost of Sample Making Process for One Style: Overseas Factory					
	Wages per day	1.5 days per sample	Overhead: 2.9 times labor	CM Total	Material & Trim	FOB Price
First sample	$9.62	$14.42	$41.83	$56.25	$7.00	$63.25
2 duplicates						$126.50
Total cost before designer approval for style going into production						$189.75
Cost of sample making process for two styles that are rejected and never produced						
2 Styles @ $189.75 per style						$379.50
Total sample making cost chargeable for one style going into production						
3 @ $189.75						$569.25

   e. Cost per piece (based on $0.50 profit per piece as shown on Basic Cost Sheet)

Chapter 5 Extrinsic Cost Savings

Order Quantity	1000	5000	10000
Sample cost per piece	$0.57	$0.11	$0.06
Percentage of profit	114%	22%	12%

2. Quantify the cost of sample making in the customer's home country:

   a. Assume a worker is paid $225 per day calculated on the basis $3300 per month for a 22-day month;
   b. Assume overhead equals 100% of labor;
   c. Assume each sample requires 1.5 man days, the same as the factory listed above;
   d. Assume sample requirements the same as the factory shown above;
      i. First sample cost
      ii. Two samples before designer approval
      iii. Two samples rejected

Cost of Sample Making Process for One Style: Customer's Home Country						
	Wages per day	1.5 days per sample	Overhead 2.9 times labor	CM Total	Material & Trim	FOB Price
First Sample	$150	$225	$225	$450	$7.00	$457
2 Duplicates						$914
Total cost before designer approval for style going into production						$1371
Cost of sample making process for two styles that are rejected and never produced						
2 Styles @ $189.75 per style						$2722
Total sample making cost chargeable for one style going into production						
3 @ $189.75						$4113

   e. Cost per piece

Order Quantity	1000	5000	10000
Sample cost per piece	$4.11	$0.82	$0.41

3. Calculate the customer savings after allowing for added factory cost plus added factory profit for sample making. Allocate the savings between the parties based on 5000 piece orders (86% for the customer and 14% for the factory).

Based on 5000 units:
- Sample cost per unit to the customer in home country = $0.82
- Added cost if factory making the sample = $0.11
- Difference of $0.71 allocated:
  - Factory = $0.10
  - Customer = $0.61

The Guide to Cost-to-Value Analysis

	Sample Making Transferred from Customer to Factory			
	Customer Sample Making		Factory Sample Making	
		Cost	Cost	
Fabric		$6.00	$6.00	
Trim		$1.00	$1.00	
CM Labor		$0.64	$0.64	
CM Overhead		$1.86	$1.86	
Added Cost Sample Making		$0.82	$0.11	
Added Factory Profit		$0.00	$0.10	
CM Total Cost		$3.32	$2.61	
Total Cost		$10.32	$9.71	
Factory Profit	5.0%	$0.50	$0.60	6.0%
Total FOB Cost		$10.82	$10.41	
Customer Savings			$0.61	

The introduction of services is but a first step whereby the factory creates greater value by reducing the customer's cost. In this instance all cost factors – for material, trims and CM – still remain unchanged. Going forward in this book, we will examine areas where the factory can create greater value by further reducing customer costs.

Transferring sample making from the customer to the factory provides several other advantages which ultimately may be greater than increased direct profit for both sides. The first advantage revolves around Quality Assurance (QA) which is a serious potential problem for the customer. Even when the first sample is approved, there is no guarantee that the factory will be able to produce a garment equivalent to the sample. This is what we call DESIGN INTEGRITY whereby the factory approval duplicate looks like the original designer sample and the stock garment looks like the factory approval duplicate. Moving down to a zero-service factory increases the risk of lost designer integrity, while the move up to a full-service factory obviates that risk.

In addition to the direct savings of 61¢ per unit, lead times are reduced. It is well known that factories can carry out the entire sample making process faster than the customer. There are simply more qualified staff with greater knowledge and experience in garment making at the factory.

Chapter 6
Calculating Value of Soft Services

The purpose of this book is to define costs and to calculate costs compared to value. In each instance the factory must be able to calculate the cost of each service and the value of that service. Where value is greater than cost, both the factory and customer benefit.

For example, as we have already seen, when the factory is located in a duty-free zone, the added cost of using local fabric rather than imported Chinese fabric is more than offset by the benefit to the customer from the eventual duty-free import of the finished garment. When the factory carries out sample making, the added CM cost is more than offset by the benefit to the customer of the reduced price of samples made by factory. Similarly, when the factory provides pick & pack redistribution services, the added cost of this service is more than offset by the savings achieved by outsourcing the work to the factory because the factory, having multiple customers, has the advantage of economies of scale.

In each case where factory costs are less than customer costs, the remaining net value provides areas of increased profits to both customer and factory.

But there are what we will call SOFT SERVICES where the cost is calculable but not the value. This applies to investments where there is potential value which has not yet been realized. When we calculated the added cost of the investment in high-tech machinery, we knew the cost ($250,000) as well as the value based on the number of workers that could be replaced by each machine. We accepted that the machine would actually work and deliver as specified.

But when we know the cost, but not the future benefit, we often do not know at all if there will be any benefit in the long run. At best we can only assume there will be a potential benefit but until that benefit has been realized, we cannot calculate the value of our investment. Nowhere is the balance between potential and realized value more apparent than when customers and suppliers invest in industrial development. The move offshore to build branch factories always carries a risk. When the new factory is located in a country with a new export garment industry, that risk rises to the level where the value of the investment is only potential.

Let us compare two examples of recent offshore industrial development, the first in Ethiopia and the second in Myanmar.

Case Study Ethiopia

This country has undeniable great potential beginning with the low cost of electricity at 3.5¢/kwh. In many respects Ethiopia is the textile/garment industry version of the discovery of oil in Saudi Arabia in 1938.

The Guide to Cost-to-Value Analysis

Africa has an abundance of cotton and it is only natural that local cotton be used to produce cotton fabric and cotton garments. But usually the obstacle to this logic is the high cost of electricity. The first step to building a viable textile industry is spinning whose single greatest cost (after the cotton) is electricity. At 3.5¢/kwh Ethiopia offers perhaps the world's lowest cost electricity, with the result that Ethiopia could potentially become the center of a major cotton textile/garment industry.

But Ethiopia also presents definite problems:

- Landlocked country
- No existing garment industry before foreign investors built branch factories
- No educated management
- No trained workers
- Poor logistics

Regardless of the problems, over the past decade, Ethiopia's export garment industry has advanced fairly rapidly, particularly to the U.S., albeit from a very low base.

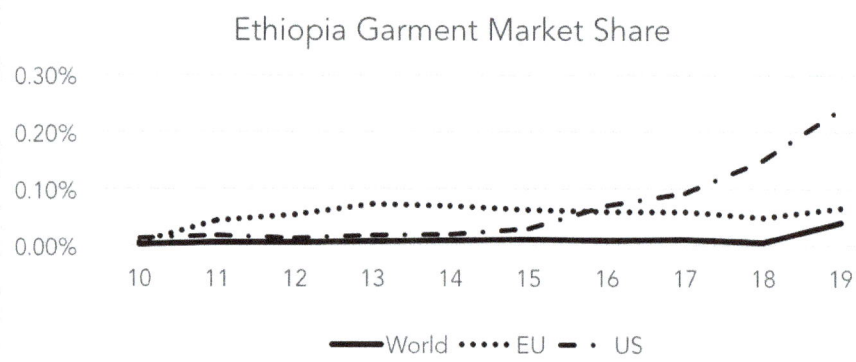

(USD thousands)   *Source: ITC*

Clearly Ethiopia is a case where it is too early to calculate the real value of investment:

- Projects might well take 20 years before showing a profit;
- Costs may run into the billions;
- Political risks are great.

Until the factories become profitable, the benefits cannot be quantified and can only be considered as potential.

Chapter 6 Calculating Value of Soft Services

Case Study Myanmar

The advantage offered by Ethiopia – cheap electricity – is real, tangible and quantifiable. If Ethiopia fails, that failure will be the result of political and social problems. Again this situation is similar to that faced by foreign investors in the oil business. But the difference is that the oil companies had greater knowledge and skill sets to assess political risk.

\multicolumn{4}{c}{Myanmar Top 20 Garment Export Products}
HTS	Product Description	Value	% Share
620520	Men's or boys' shirts of cotton	277,200	17.6%
620339	Men's or boys' jackets and blazers other than 100% cotton, wool or synthetic	243,337	15.4%
620349	Men's or boys' trousers, other than 100% cotton, wool or synthetics.	209,197	13.3%
620439	Women's or girls' jackets and blazers other than 100% cotton, wool or synthetic	39,064	2.5%
620333	Men's or boys' jackets and blazers of synthetic fibres	33,974	2.2%
620630	Women's or girls' blouses, of cotton	32,856	2.1%
620462	Women's or girls' trousers of cotton	31,560	2.0%
621210	Brassieres	30,772	2.0%
620690	Women's or girls' blouses, other than 100% cotton, wool or synthetic	28,780	1.8%
620311	Men's or boys' suits of wool	28,512	1.8%
621120	Ski suits	28,114	1.8%
620312	Men's or boys' suits of synthetic fibres	18,163	1.2%
620319	Men's or boys' suits of other than 100% cotton, wool or synthetic	16,782	1.1%
610290	Women's or girls' coats other than 100% cotton, wool or synthetic	16,525	1.0%
620930	Babies' garments and clothing accessories of synthetic fibres	15,961	1.0%
611490	Special garments for professional, sporting or other purposes	13,047	0.8%
620341	Men's or boys' trousers of wool	10,607	0.7%
610822	Women's or girls' briefs and panties of manmade fibres, knitted or crocheted	10,577	0.7%
620419	Women's or girls' suits of other than 100% cotton, wool or synthetic	8,332	0.5%
620469	Women's or girls' trousers, other than 100% cotton, wool or synthetic	7,238	0.5%

Source: ITC

The Guide to Cost-to-Value Analysis

The table above shows how Myanmar is different. While foreigners must build the Ethiopian garment industry from the ground up, Myanmar already had an existing garment industry with a pool of skilled workers. Furthermore, as we can see from the chart below, Myanmar's industry is not in the cheap commodity garment business.

Because of sanctions, from 2003-2010, garment exports from Myanmar were sharply curtailed. The end of sanctions placed Myanmar in the unique position of being a new industry which did not have to go through the usual long period of development from t-shirts and underwear to more complex products. If the customer wanted men's suits, women's coats or skiwear, Myanmar was ready to produce and deliver from Day 1.

Nevertheless, the downside of working in Myanmar is also politics. Customers recall the events in 2003 where Myanmar was cast as an outlaw nation. Now many fear that because of politics, working in Myanmar might become difficult again. This time the decisions to not buy made-in-Myanmar garments might not come from customers and be the result of government policies but from end consumers who refuse to buy made-in-Myanmar because they don't support the Myanmar government.

So far customers remain optimistic. Despite the potential political problems, between 2015-2017, Myanmar exports to the world increased substantially.

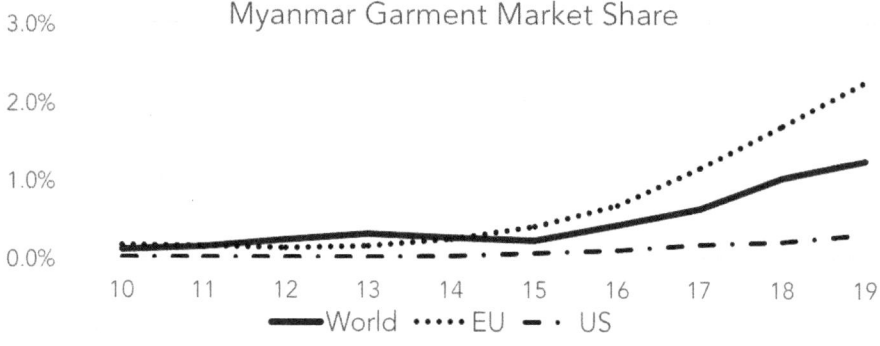

(USD thousands) *Source: ITC*

Myanmar market share of under 2.5% to the EU and 0.5% to the U.S. for 2019 is still very low. This is not true of Japan where Myanmar accounted for 7.7% of Japan's global garment imports in 2018 and is its third largest supplier after China and Vietnam.

Chapter 6 Calculating Value of Soft Services

(USD thousands) *Source: ITC*

The question remains, have customers' investments in Myanmar moved from potential to manifest? From the current data, it would appear that the value derived from Myanmar is real and quantifiable. But we should not rush to judgement just yet. Investments in Myanmar are so far limited to the individual factory level. If customers see a deteriorating situation, they can pull out almost overnight. Contrast this with Ethiopia, where foreign direct investment is substantial and growing and where pulling out would be costly for all.

In short, for the time being, the value of garment industry investments in both Ethiopia and Myanmar must be relegated to the SOFT SERVICES category because the benefits, if any, cannot be quantified.

Chapter 7
Negative Value Soft Services

In our consumer-dominated market, brands and retailers all work first to understand consumer demands and then to meet those demands. Everyone understands that following consumer demands is not only the necessary road to success but also the necessary way to avoid failure.

Consumers want clothes that incorporate good design, good make and are available at the best price. These are all areas of positive value. If you are a brand or retailer and meet these demands, there is a good chance the consumer will buy your merchandise.

But consumers also make demands that have negative value. These are areas where meeting these demands will not necessarily result in increased sales, but where failure to meet them will certainly result in decreased sales not only for the brands and retailers but also for their factory suppliers. These areas also fall in the category of soft services. But we can quantify only the negative value, the loss that ensues from the failure to provide those services. There is no real way to relate cost to positive value.

Number one on the list of negative value is Corporate Social Responsibility (CSR), particularly for millennials and post-millennials. These younger consumers are not only an already important sector, but they will become increasingly important as older consumers die off. Sustainability, transparency and compliance are already becoming the most important factors in determining who on the supplier side will NOT get the order and who on the customer side will NOT get the sale.

It would seem obvious that if the consumer wants CSR standards to be met, then everyone on both the customer and supplier sides should be working hard to provide meaningful CSR. Unfortunately this is currently not the case.

On the positive side, many companies see CSR to be of primary importance. Some have always had a culture of ethical behavior; their customers have always believed in ethical sourcing and work with suppliers that have built zero-carbon-footprint factories. Other companies have more recently seen the light and adopted CSR. Sometimes these newcomers become zealous converts, anxious to convert the entire world.

The move towards CSR is indeed growing but as of yet still constitutes a minority of companies on both the customer and supplier sides. On the negative side, there are those who think of CSR as an advertising gimmick, something to stick on a hangtag even if the company doesn't really apply the standards. Even here there is an upside. Those who dishonestly claim to follow ethical standards must still believe that the market considers CSR important, or why bother lying.

The Guide to Cost-to-Value Analysis

Unfortunately, senior executives at many companies still take the position that CSR compliance is nonsense. Their argument is that although consumers say they care about CSR, may sign petitions favoring CSR and even picket stores found guilty of unethical behavior, at the end of the day, CSR is irrelevant to what they will buy. The vast majority of consumers buy clothing on the basis of design, fit, make and price. This position has a great deal of support from economists, sociologists and most particularly, big data specialists.

Nevertheless, this conclusion does not make sense. Take, for example, child labor and assume that only 10% of consumers are truly against child labor. The other 90% do not favor child labor; instead they simply do not care. It is relatively easy for those in the industry to jump on the bandwagon and oppose child labor. Even if 90% of consumers do not care, suppliers and customers alike have to support the 10% who do care, because those who do care will not buy the garments produced by 10-year-old children, while the other 90% do not care one way or another.

I have come across a similar case in litigation between garment importers and tax authorities where I have been retained as an industry expert. The same argument has been used by government tax authorities who maintain that companies are not entitled to tax benefits for work carried out for CSR because that work brings neither increased sales nor added profit. They say that consumers do not care about sustainability, the ecology or working conditions. They might sign petitions. They might even picket stores, but at the end of the day their buying decisions have little to do with social responsibility. When buying clothing, the consumer looks for design, fit, price and even quality. When buying food, the consumer cares about taste, look and price. Most consumers do not care about nutrition. Think Big Macs and Krispy Kreme.

The tax authorities have mountains of data to "prove" their point. During litigation, they bring in their ten experts – economists, accountants and big data mavens – while the importers bring in theirs. Eventually the judge is handed some 2000 pages of data and is left to decide the relative merits of each side. Who is more credible – the tenured professor from MIT or the tenured professor from Stanford, the Nobel Prize winner or the Fields Medal winner? One thing is clear, lacking in PhD degrees in any of the relevant disciplines, the judge is not qualified to express any opinion.

There is an alternate argument, one that does not require 2000 pages or 20 experts, but only two pages and a single expert that the judge respects the most. It is about reality. Data is of great value until the moment it is contradicted by reality.

The Case of the Angora Rabbit

Angora sweaters was an important product for well over 100 years. An angora sweater was soft, fluffy and warm. Prices were very competitive because most

Chapter 7 Negative Value of Soft Services

angora sweaters were made of blended yarn. Today that product no longer exists. This story is all about rabbits. Different cultures look at rabbits differently. In Australia they shoot rabbits as vermin. In Europe they eat rabbits as Italian Coniglio, German Hasenpfeffer and French Lapin à la Cocotte. Americans are different. To us rabbits are Flopsy, Mopsy, Cottontail and Peter. My children were bought up with the Velveteen Rabbit. We all know and love the Easter Bunny. A few years ago, an animal rights NGO published a detailed report showing how we get the hair off the Easter Bunny. Think medieval torture. The day after the report was published the market for angora sweaters died. The angora sweater is still soft, fluffy, warm and now cheap. It has everything except customers.

The Case of Healthy Food

For years we were told by supposedly knowledgeable experts that natural food was a fad, limited to the wealthy. Most people did not care about healthy food. Think how widespread obesity is becoming. There was only one naysayer. Jeff Bezos believed that demand for healthy food was elastic. People wanted to eat healthier food but could not afford the prices charged by Whole Foods and the other natural food retailers. In the end, Mr. Bezos bought Whole Foods and then dropped their prices by 35%. The question remains: Who do you believe – tenured professors, Nobel Prize or Fields Medal winners, or the world's most successful retailer?

The main advantage of dealing in the real world rather than the world of big data is that in the real world we have access to more reliable if not to say more trustworthy experts. In our case, the judge can go home to obtain a truly expert opinion – from his wife.

Judge: Sarah, tell me about angora sweaters.

Wife: What's to tell? I used to have one or two. Your mother, may she rest in peace, had many. I stopped wearing them because the stores stopped selling them. I actually asked. The saleswoman told me they stopped selling angora sweaters because they were receiving complaints from some of their customers.

Judge: Sarah, tell me about natural food.

Sarah: What are you going on about? Do I go into your court, do you want to go into my shopping? Everybody knows that good health is the greatest wealth. I have been putting healthy natural food on the table for the past 25 years. I have noticed that now when I go to Whole Foods, they seem to have many new customers, people who I never thought cared about healthy food. I think the lower prices makes a difference. Cousin Rachel tells me that her husband Fred believes the old grocery stores are in shtuck.

Case closed!

The Guide to Cost-to-Value Analysis

Humor aside, there are two important points to be made here:

1. Corporate social responsibility is not a myth nor is it simply charity. CSR is a valuable business strategy aimed at providing value to the consumer as perceived by the consumer.

2. Data is an important tool but reality always trumps data.

Chapter 8
Cost vs Price

Cost is what the supplier pays. Everything has a cost and that cost is quantifiable. We may not know the cost. We may forget to add the cost of a particular item to our cost sheet. Nevertheless, our failure to add the cost of the zipper to our cost sheet does not reduce the cost of the garment. It just makes our cost sheet inaccurate.

Price is what the customer pays. It is not quantifiable because the amount the customer pays is based on value. Therefore, any attempt to relate price to cost (price = cost plus+) although commonly accepted by the U.S. Department of Defense almost invariably leads to irrational conclusions, such as the $2400 screwdriver, the $24,000 toilet seat and, more recently, the $24,000,000 refrigerator.

For the rest of us, both people and companies, the decision to buy is based on the ratio between value and price. When the value is greater than price, we buy. When the value falls below price, we do not buy. Value is personal. It may not be rational, but it is real.

Case Study V: Buying a Porsche

The price of a Porsche is $100,000. If you have a $100,000 and want to buy a Porsche, you buy the Porsche. You do not care what the Porsche people paid for material and production. Your reason for paying $100,000 to buy a car need not be rational.

You might have grown up in a modest-income family. Each day you rode to school on your secondhand bike, while Richie Rich zoomed past you, his father driving him in a brand new Porsche.

So it was that at the age of 12, you decided that one day having achieved success you would own a brand new Porsche. Why you bought your Porsche is a matter between you and your therapist. Another person might think you are crazy to buy a Porsche, when for the same amount of money, you could have bought a first-class Persian carpet.

The difference between price and cost is one of the most important factors determining factory success or failure.

Clearly, if everything has a cost, the EVERYTHING must also include the intangibles, such as quality, reliability, and reduced lead times. We can quantify these costs at least indirectly because factories capable of providing those intangibles as a rule will charge a higher price. However, using the basic cost sheet we cannot calculate the value of these items to the customer because those areas of value

The Guide to Cost-to-Value Analysis

simply do not exist on our cost sheet.

Once we accept that the intangibles do not appear on our cost sheets, we are forced to accept one of two possible mutually exclusive conclusions which are fundamental to the whole question of costings and cost sheets:

      A. Intangibles such as quality, reliability and reduced lead times have no value; or

      B. Our entire methodology of cost sheets is irrevocably flawed.

Don't kid yourself, choosing between these two conclusions is not obvious. For over 30 years, our entire industry voted for A, and even now, major brands and retailers still vote for A. This is what we term the COMPETITIVE MODEL. Now as our industry evolves into the later models, the customer side is beginning to recognize the importance of the intangibles.

Strategic Suppliers

Where once factories were defined only as product makers, customers now recognize that more qualified factories can be service suppliers. The move from zero-service to full-service supplier has separated the supply side into two groups: the replaceable supplier and the strategic supplier. Not only can the strategic supplier charge more, but he can avoid SEASONALITY, the bane of garment factories everywhere. Our industry is to a large degree controlled by climate. We have high seasons and low seasons. We have cold weather clothing. We have warm weather clothing. We even have clothing for those people who want to escape from their local climate and take a holiday in places with a different climate.

In a world without seasons, every factory would produce 8.333% of its annual production each month. The graph below shows the actual monthly average of world imports for the period 2013-2017. As you can see, the year begins with imports at world average (8.333%) which represents the arrival of spring season garments. It then falls each month until reaching a trough in April, rising again as fall season garments begin to arrive, finally reaching a peak in August, after which it slowly begins to decline again.

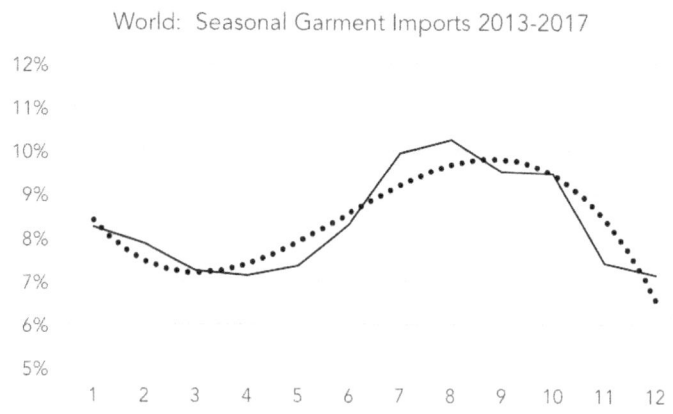

Source: ITC

Chapter 8 Cost vs Price

Some factories are able to escape seasonality because they provide added value such that their customers have a vested interest in securing their production. These are the strategic suppliers. In order to secure production space, customers must guarantee constant orders both high season and low season. As the industry has developed, customers have ever greater need for suppliers capable of providing greater services, which in turn has increased their need for more full-service factories. As the number of strategic suppliers increases, the problems of seasonality for non-strategic suppliers worsens. If 50% of all garment orders were given to strategic suppliers, the overall peaks and troughs remain unaltered, but variations become far more extreme for non-strategic suppliers. This graph illustrates this situation:

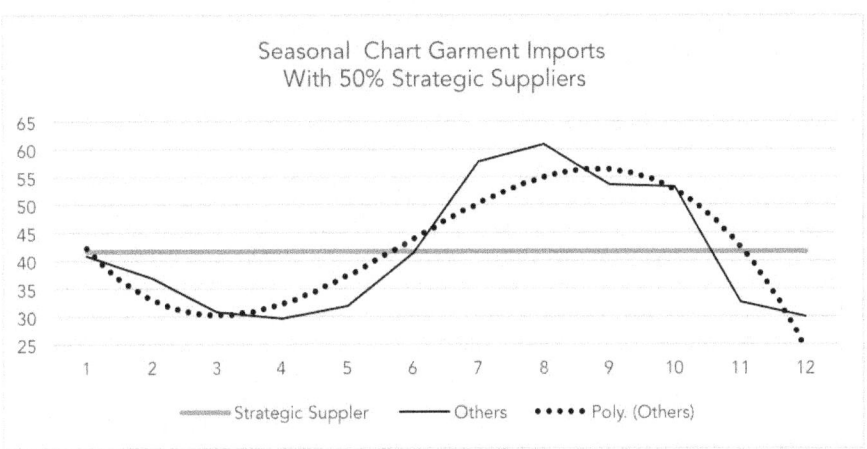

Peak vs Trough Months 2013-2017			
	Peak	Trough	
World without Strategic Suppliers	Aug	Apr	
	10.3%	7.1%	44.0%
World with Strategic Suppliers	Aug	Mar	
	61	30	105.9%

In the world without strategic suppliers the difference between high and low season is 44%. In that same world where 50% of orders are placed with strategic suppliers that difference grows to 106%. Unless your factory is a strategic supplier to someone, survival becomes very difficult. Clearly every factory wants to be at least someone's strategic supplier.

There are three factors any one of which will allow a factory to become a strategic supplier:

- Product
- Quality
- Service

The Guide to Cost-to-Value Analysis

Product

Product type: At the low end of the scale are factories producing basic commodities such as t-shirts, jeans and underwear. It is almost impossible for the basic commodity factory to become an important supplier, let alone a strategic supplier, because at any given time there are more suppliers than customers.

Producing a special product is a way to become a strategic supplier. At the high end of the product scale there are what in the industry we call the PRODUCTS FROM HELL. These are products so bizarre that there are very few competent producers, with the result that if you are a customer importing one of the products from hell, and you have a good supplier, the best way, and the least expensive way, to keep that supplier is to guarantee steady business.

Here are some examples:

Bridalwear: In the past when couples got married, the bridal gown was a major status symbol and designers piled on increasing layers of fabric and tchotchkes and embellishment. Very few factories could operate at the necessary level when designers were competing with one another to create the world's first totally unproduceable product.

Bras: Imagine a product that requires three materials, two lace inserts, satin trim, a bow and two elastics. Everything must be dyed to match, then cut and sewn in 100+ sizes. That is what a bra factory must do.

Girls dresses 6-16: The CM on a girl's dress is about the same as a dress for her mother. But of course the customer will not pay the same CM. Furthermore, where the woman's dress factory only has to produce and ship dresses, the importer of Size 6-16 girls' dresses requires much more: matching shoes, hand bag, and a letter of acceptance to a leading private elementary school.

Quality

Every customer says they want the best quality but most have no idea of what constitutes the best quality and even fewer are willing to pay. Those factories at the very top of the quality tree are potential strategic suppliers.

Chapter 8   Cost vs Price

> Case Study VI: The World's Greatest Factory (slightly exaggerated)
>
> A small factory (80 machines) located in France produced very high-quality women's tailored jackets, skirts and pants. Their customers were some of the best designers in the world. Accordingly, their prices were very high: a jacket averaged CM $80-$120. Unfortunately, their customers had only two seasons, meaning for the six months of high season orders, the factory did very well indeed, but for rest of the year, they pretty much lost all the profit from the high season.
>
> Eventually the factory brought in a consultant. The consultant's first step was to carry out cost analysis, creating job cost sheets for a certain number of styles. He recognized that in France a factory could not lay off workers. That meant that during low season, losses came from more than just overhead but also included wages and therefore the entirety of what the factory would have earned from CM had they had orders.
>
> The consultant's next step was to determine the breakeven point where CM prices charged to the customer would equal annual CM cost. Finally the consultant designed a workable strategy to return the factory to profit. The plan he submitted called for doubling the size of the factory from 80 to 160 machines. To the factory management and its owners, doubling the size of a money-losing factory seemed insane.
>
> The consultant reasoned that to the right U.S. importer, the combination of ultimate high quality together with a made-in-France label would definitely define the factory as a strategic supplier. Consequently during high season when the factory had orders from their regular couture customers, the U.S. importer would provide orders for 80 machines and for low season, orders for all 160 machines. After all, even 160 machines would not produce all that many high-end garments.
>
> The only question was to determine a CM price agreeable to both parties which worked out to be $40-$50 per unit. At that level the factory was able to cover the cost of labor and about 65% of overhead. Yes, it still lost money during low season, but the losses were sharply reduced, substantially increasing net profit for the year.

In a sense we can understand why factories capable of dealing with the products from hell or those providing truly exceptional quality are entitled to special consideration. But those special factories account for at best 1% of all garment suppliers. The question remains, what can the other 99% do to join the strategic supplier elite.

Services

Where once garment factories were simply product makers, those at the cutting edge had to become service suppliers and, in doing so, created increased value

The Guide to Cost-to-Value Analysis

which entitled them to charge higher prices. Let's look at what a comparison cost sheet with and without added services would look like.

Basic Cost Sheet with or without Added Services				
	No Added Services		With Added Services	
		Cost	Cost	
Fabric	60.0%	$6.00	$6.00	60.0%
Trim	10.0%	$1.00	$1.00	10.0%
CM Labor	6.4%	$0.64	$0.64	6.4%
CM Overhead	18.6%	$1.86	$1.86	18.6%
CM Total Cost	25.0%	$2.50	$2.50	25.0%
Total Cost	95.0%	$9.50	$9.50	95.0%
Factory Profit	5.0%	$0.50	$0.50	5.0%
Total FOB Cost	100.0%	$10.00	$10.00	100.0%

What you immediately realize if you look at the figures above with or without added services, the numbers are exactly the same. Services are nowhere to be found in the basic cost sheet but are indeed locked somewhere in overhead. this results in two serious problems:

- We do not know the cost of each service.
- The cost per unit for services is materially different than cost per unit for labor or overheard.

This second problem is particularly important. We define labor and overhead costs on a per unit basis neither of which are affected by the size of the order. Labor cost for our garment is 64¢ and overhead $1.86 per piece regardless of the size of the order. We can argue that productivity on a style rises as the size of the order increases, thus decreasing the cost per unit. This is undoubtedly true when we compare an order for 2000 pieces with an order for the same style of 1,000,000 pieces. But in the real world the factory producing 2000 pieces will not be the same factory producing 1,000,000 pieces.

Services, on the other hand, are very different. As we saw previously in our analysis of sample making services, the cost of sample making for a style on the factory side is $569.25. Therefore the cost per unit is inversely proportional to the size of the order: the cost per unit for an order of 1000 pieces is 57¢, for 5000 pieces 11¢ and for 10,000 pieces only 6¢.

These are substantial differences which must somehow be reflected in the cost sheets. The benefit of value-added services offered by the supplier is so great to customer and supplier alike that we must change our system of cost sheets to quantify both the costs and the value of each service.

Chapter 9
The Incomplete Cost Sheet

At the risk of repeating yet again, everything is about cost. Costs are quantifiable. But if a particular item is not included in the factory's cost sheet, the cost sheet cannot be reconciled to the actual cost. To take a simple example, if the price of the zipper is not included in the cost sheet, the total material cost will appear to be lower than the real cost.

The move from garment buying to garment sourcing has taken away the factory's ability to control its own costs. The customer has already purchased the material and has designated the trim. At the same time, the customer has specified fabric consumption and number of minutes required to produce the garment based on past experience and productivity from that region. At first it would appear that in this open-sourcing world, the order will go to the factory offering the lowest cost per minute presumably in the countries with the lowest incomes. This is truly the race to the bottom.

Yet export figures in this millennium show this assumption to be demonstrably untrue. If we consider the largest garment-exporting countries, we see that five of the top ten are high-income Western European countries and two – China and Turkey – are middle-income. Together these seven countries account for over half of world garment exports and three times the exports from the remaining top ten – Bangladesh, Vietnam and India – who are low-income countries.

	Top 10 Garment-Exporting Countries 2001-2017									
	Rank	01	03	05	07	09	11	13	15	17
Italy	4	7.1%	6.9%	6.6%	6.3%	5.8%	5.3%	4.9%	4.4%	4.7%
Germany	5	3.8%	4.1%	4.4%	4.4%	5.2%	4.9%	4.2%	3.8%	4.6%
Spain	8	1.1%	1.5%	1.6%	1.7%	2.3%	2.2%	2.5%	2.7%	3.0%
France	9	2.8%	3.0%	2.9%	3.0%	2.9%	2.5%	2.3%	2.2%	2.4%
Netherlands	10	1.3%	1.4%	1.4%	1.6%	1.8%	2.0%	1.9%	1.6%	1.9%
High Income		16.1%	16.9%	16.8%	17.0%	18.1%	16.8%	15.8%	14.8%	16.6%
China	1	17.5%	20.5%	24.5%	31.8%	31.8%	35.2%	37.6%	37.0%	32.1%
Turkey	7	3.4%	4.3%	4.3%	3.9%	3.5%	3.3%	3.4%	3.4%	3.3%
Middle Income		20.9%	24.8%	28.7%	35.8%	35.3%	38.5%	41.0%	40.4%	35.4%
Bangladesh	2	2.2%	2.3%	2.5%	2.7%	3.9%	4.7%	4.5%	6.0%	7.7%
Vietnam	3	1.0%	1.5%	1.7%	2.1%	2.6%	3.1%	3.8%	4.9%	5.4%
India	6	2.7%	2.7%	3.0%	2.7%	3.6%	3.4%	3.6%	3.9%	3.8%
Low Income		5.9%	6.4%	7.3%	7.6%	10.1%	11.2%	11.9%	14.8%	16.9%

Sources: ITC calculations based on UN Comtrade and ITC statistics

The Guide to Cost-to-Value Analysis

Clearly we need to look closer at what these figures are telling us.

> Case Study VII: A Pail of Water
>
> A teacher, introducing his class to algebra, provides a demonstration. How do we do we calculate the time necessary to fill a pail of water? If we label the pail's capacity as X, and the rate of flow of water into the pail as Y, the number of minutes C required to fill the pail to capacity is X/Y=C.
>
> The teacher then goes on to demonstrate the formula. He takes a pail with a capacity of 16oz (X=16) and proceeds to fill it at the rate of 4oz per minute (Y=4) to show that the pail would be filled to capacity in precisely four minutes 16/4=4. Unfortunately, the pail requires six minutes to reach capacity and does so each time the teacher repeats the experiment.
>
> The teacher is very disturbed and therefore travels to the local university to determine just what went wrong. Perhaps the problem was due to evaporation. He brings in a climatologist who explains that the problem cannot be evaporation. Four minutes is too short a period to allow for appreciable loss due to evaporation, and furthermore, given that the experiment has taken place in Thule Greenland, the rate of evaporation would be reduced even further.
>
> Perhaps the problem is due to a chemical reaction between the water and pail. He brings in a chemist who explains that the problem cannot be oxidation. Four minutes is too short a period to allow the pail to rust, and furthermore, the fact that the pail is made of stainless steel would reduce oxidation even further.
>
> The teacher becomes more and more desperate and calls in other experts including a cosmologist – perhaps the problem is caused by black matter passing through the solar system – and a quantum physicist – perhaps the problem is caused by an aberration in our understanding of multidimensional string theory. All to no avail.
>
> In the end, totally at a loss to explain the additional two minutes, the teacher takes the pail home where he attempts over and over again to repeat the experiment until his eight-year-old son notes that the pail has a hole at the bottom.

The basic cost sheet has a hole at the bottom. It is missing one or more factors which when added to the cost sheet would show why exports from high-income countries equal exports from low-income countries and exports from middle-income countries are greater than the total of exports from both low and high-income countries. Or to put it another way, why China offers something to its importer customers that is worth over four times exports from Bangladesh.

Chapter 9   The Incomplete Cost Sheet

As I wrote earlier, to increase profit the factory must go through a two-step process:

1. Determine what are these value-added services that customers will pay more for.
2. Ensure the costs for those value-added services are included in the cost sheet.

Everything has a cost and a value. Often the cost relates to something tangible, such as we saw in the case of sample making. Sometimes that cost is intangible which makes cost vs. value calculations extremely difficult and often counterproductive.

Let's look at quality. While quality is one of the most important factors in garment production, its quantification is often totally miscalculated.

Case Study VIII: A Tale of Two Factories

Imagine two factories: Mr. Good Factory and Mr. Garbage Pail.

Mr. Good Factory ships a fine product, on time, every time. When visiting his factory the customer's QC inspectors have little to do. They go through the motions, while the QC team's manager sits in Mr. Good Factory's office drinking tea and discusses local politics and, more importantly, the latest cricket scandal. When the customer's buying office is in trouble because a style is difficult to the point where it is beyond the capability of other factory suppliers, they know that Mr. Good Factory will step in to save the day. Yes, Mr. Good Factory's CM is higher than others, but the value far outweighs the cost.

Mr. Garbage Pail is at the other end of the spectrum. He can ship a good product, on time, provided it is the simplest product. Provided also that the buying office sends in the QC police at 2am to ensure that the factory is not packing today's rejects for tomorrow's shipment. And provided that the buying office is willing to carry out 100% in-process inspection followed by 100% final inspection. Mr. Garbage Pail's only value is low CM and that is only possible because the buying office uses what it saves working with Mr. Good Factory to subsidize the costs of dealing with Mr. Garbage Pail.

Meanwhile the customer is keeping track of the supplying factories. He has developed a 10-point program to differentiate the best from the worst factories. The customer's people look at Mr. Garbage Pail's numbers and they like what they see. The orders are shipped on time. The quality looks good and the price is very competitive. Why, they ask, are we working with Mr. Good Factory? Yes, he ships a nice product on time, but his prices are totally out of line. Clearly the local buying office is not doing their job.

Every importer states categorically that good quality provides value. For the importer to get a higher quality product, he has to go to a better factory that naturally charges more than a not-so-good factory. We can see the cost in the

The Guide to Cost-to-Value Analysis

higher CM. There must some benefit to higher quality and if indeed everything is about cost, that benefit must not only be quantifiable, it must be seen to be worth more than the cost of the higher CM. So where is it? Here is another example of the hole-in-the-bucket cost sheet.

Case Study IX: The Gap Syndrome

Mickey Drexler is probably the greatest merchant of my generation. Certainly, in the same class as Freddy Lazarus and Sir Simon Marks. These people have some sixth sense that enables them to know precisely what their customer wants. In 1983, Gap was just one more San Francisco-based denim retailer when owner Donald Fisher hired Mickey Drexler as CEO. Drexler was very much a garment professional. He developed a plan for Gap. His new target customers were people who wanted well-designed, well-made garments but who had no interest in fashion. In pursuit of his goal he not only made Gap into the largest garment retailer in the U.S., he made non-fashion cool. This was not an easy task.

You had to be a professional to truly understand the Drexler strategy. During the 1990s, I used to travel to the U.S. for work. About twice a year, I would buy my children's wardrobe at Gap. The look was very nice, the people very professional and the quality impeccable. You could go to Gap in San Francisco and buy a navy t-shirt, then travel to Gap in New York and not only find the same t-shirt in the identical navy shade and cast, but also buy a pair of woven shorts in the identical navy shade and cast. The t-shirt might have been made in a China factory and the pants in an Indonesia factory. That was Gap then.

Mickey Drexler was a first-class manager. If you were on his team, from senior designer to shop sales assistant, you were family. For a variety of reasons, in 2002 after a relatively small sales and profit decline that was industry-wide, Gap's founder asked Mickey Drexler to leave the company.

The next CEO, although a very successful retail executive, had no garment industry experience. His first goal was to increase profits. In MBA school we are taught that retailers have three ways to increase profit:

- Increase sales volume
- Increase prices
- Reduce costs

Increasing sales volume is a long process with relatively low benefits. For every $1 increase in sales, the company earns 6¢. Increasing retail prices was a non-starter since Gap prices were already at a premium to its competitor's prices. So the new CEO decided to reduce costs.

The new management immediately recognized that product was the easiest area for cost reduction. Drexler's suppliers produced goods far better than the market demanded. Why buy from the Rolls Royce of textile mills and the Tiffany of garment factories when less expensive suppliers were ready and able to produce materials and garments of almost equal quality?

In the short term they were correct. Slightly lower quality goods had no effect on

Chapter 9   The Incomplete Cost Sheet

sales and profits increased. But as markdowns began to rise, the new management team recognized that they had a quality problem. The new management team came from the toy industry and understood the importance of quality. If your customer is a child or infant, poor quality can result in horrific problems which could put you out of business. The new management team defined quality as zero defects. Their solution was to impose increasingly stricter quality control. The buying office QC department became the QC police which in turn became the QC army. But even with QC inspectors permanently located in the factory, markdown rates continued to rise.

The garment industry is different to the toy industry. A poorly sewn pair of pants where the back seam splits may mortify the wearer but he will not die. Garment industry quality is not in itself related to damage. Gap's move to lower quality fabrics did not in itself cause damages. Moving from a t-shirt made of 97% cotton/3% spandex to a cheaper polyester blend or from 100% cashmere to 40% cashmere/60% lamb's wool yarn for sweaters or from worsted flannel to wool flannel for jackets, all reduced quality but did not cause damages.

On the factory side, moving from single-needle to double-needle shirt sewing or from fully lined to half-lined to unlined blazer jackets reduced quality but did not cause damages. Nor did moving from open-seamed to welt-seamed to 5-thread overlock seamed pants or from full fashion to overlocked seamed sweaters. Most importantly, designs were dumbed down so that zero-service factories could make the goods which certainly reduced quality. Yet none of these moves caused damages.

At the end of the day, in the garment industry, poor quality is not necessarily related to increased damages. But it is related to the reduced value that the consumer places on the garment and therefore the price the consumer is willing to pay for that garment.

Finally Gap management's inability to understand much less solve the markdown problem forced them to increase markup to the point where the first markdown brought prices back to their original full markup. If the Gap retail price was set at $10, they increased the price to $15 with the expectation that a markdown rate of 33% would bring the price back to $10. This tactic proved to be a spectacular failure. Because as almost all professionals agree, you should not try to fool the American consumer because when it comes to shopping, the U.S. is a nation of Nobel Prize winners. Naturally the consumers outwaited Gap until after the first, second and third markdown, even if they had to delay Christmas shopping until January.

Greater markdowns brought more intense QC inspection which seemed to result in even greater markdowns. While under the Drexler Regime, net retail volume was four times FOB, that figure eventually fell to 2.5 times FOB. The post-Drexler period brought a reversal in Gap's position in the industry, from which it has never recovered.

- From 1996-2005 retail volume rose by 307% while retail sales from 2006-2018 fell by 1%.
- Profits from 1996-2005 averaged 6.7% annually including a $776mn loss in 2002. Excluding that one-year loss, profits under Drexler averaged

The Guide to Cost-to-Value Analysis

8.0% compared with 6.5% for the 13 following years 2006-2018. Profit for 2016-2018 averaged 5.2%.

	Gap Sales Volume and Profit: Drexler vs Post Drexler		
	Volume $bn	Profit $bn	PCT Profit
1996	$5.300	$0.453	8.5%
1997	$6.500	$0.534	8.2%
1998	$9.100	$0.825	9.1%
1999	$11.600	$1.127	9.7%
2000	$11.635	$1.127	9.7%
2001	$13.673	$0.877	6.4%
2002	$13.847	-$0.776	-5.6%
2003	$15.900	$1.031	6.5%
2004	$16.300	$1.150	7.1%
2005	$16.267	$1.150	7.1%
2006	$16.019	$1.131	7.1%
2007	$15.923	$0.809	5.1%
2008	$15.763	$0.867	5.5%
2009	$14.526	$0.967	6.7%
2010	$14.197	$1.102	7.8%
2011	$14.664	$1.204	8.2%
2012	$15.549	$0.833	5.4%
2013	$15.651	$1.135	7.3%
2014	$16.148	$1.280	7.9%
2015	$16.435	$1.262	7.7%
2016	$15.797	$0.920	5.8%
2017	$15.516	$0.676	4.4%
2018	$15.855	$0.848	5.3%

If quality is a cost, then higher quality should bring greater value and greater value higher price. This is true for both the customer and his supplier. This is also true whether quality appears or does not appear on your cost sheet. The Gap epic is a prime example of a poor cost sheet where the company saw no value in quality and paid a heavy price for their mistake.

Chapter 10
Full Value Cost Sheet

For many years factories and importers alike relied on the basic cost sheet as their sourcing and negotiating tool. This was based on two assumptions:

- That fabric, trim and CM were the sole responsibilities of the supplier;
- That FOB was the single most important factor for success. The factory offering the lowest FOB price would receive the order.

As we have seen, neither assumption was correct. Relatively early on, fabric and trim ceased to be the responsibility of the factory. As importers moved from garment buying to garment sourcing, the importers themselves negotiated price directly with the fabric mills and trim suppliers, leaving the factory with only the responsibility of paying the materials suppliers at the previously agreed price.

Without responsibility for fabric and trim, all negotiations between customer and supplier devolved around CM (labor-overhead-factory profit). Even this more limited area proved to be inaccurate. In the short run both direct labor and overhead costs are beyond the control of factory management. When the buyer demands a CM price reduction, the factory boss cannot go to his workers and ask them to take a wage cut; nor can he telephone the electric company asking for a reduced electric bill just because business is not going well. In fact, net profit is the only area where the factory can reduce what they get from their prices.

In this new environment CM in itself is no longer an indication of anything. Low CM might indicate a successful factory with high productivity or alternatively a failing factory unable to get business at profitable prices. At the same time high CM can both indicate a successful factory able to provide important services to its customers or a failing factory no longer able to offer competitive prices.

FOB price has also become meaningless. A customer may consider a high FOB price to be a bargain from one factory and outrageously high from another factory, all depending on the product, the services and the reliability of the factory.

The basic cost sheet has two additional failures:

a. The basic cost sheet fails to include many of the major garment costs. As we have seen earlier, for years customers failed to recognize the cost savings that could be derived from reduced tariffs when purchasing fabric from within the free-trade area even when the price of that fabric was higher than from a third-party country. What is true of fabric sourcing is equally true of potential cost reductions derived from transferring product development from the customer to the factory or, most importantly, factory services that help reduce markdowns.

The Guide to Cost-to-Value Analysis

In every case the problem is because the specific item – import tariff, product development, markdown – has not been included in the cost sheet.

b. The basic cost sheet fails to differentiate FOB cost from FOB price. As we in the industry have learned over many years, cost (what the factory pays) and price (what the customer pays) are not synonymous. They are not even related. Only a cost sheet which includes both is truly useful.

The full value cost sheet is a tool that overcomes these deficiencies. It recognizes that the factory can play an important role in areas previously considered to be outside its purview and therefore includes all of the costs, from the very beginning of the traditional supply chain PRODUCT DEVELOPMENT to the final IN-STORE DELIVERY OF STOCK MERCHANDISE and even beyond, to LAST PIECE SOLD.

The full value cost sheet also differentiates cost from price. As we have learned, cost and price are unrelated. Cost – what the factory pays for materials and CM – is quantifiable. Price – what the customer pays – is related to value. Every new service provided by the factory brings added cost. To be successful the value provided to the customer by that service must be greater than the added cost. Below is an example of a full value cost sheet.

Chapter 10 Full Value Cost Sheet

		Full Value Cost Sheet			
			No Added Services	With Added Services	
				Cost	Price	
1	Material		$6.00	$6.00	
2	Trim		$1.00	$1.00	
3	CM Labor		$0.64	$0.64	
4	CM Overhead		$1.86	$1.86	
5	CM Total Cost		$2.50	$2.50	
6	Total Cost		$9.50	$9.50	
7	Factory Profit		$0.50	$0.50	
8	Total FOB Cost		$10.00	$10.00	
9	Agent Commission	5.0%	$0.50	$0.50	5.0%
10	Freight		$0.25	$0.25	
11	Duty	16.2%	$1.62	$1.62	16.2%
12	Clearance		$0.10	$0.10	
13	Transport		$0.15	$0.15	
14	Total DDP		$12.62	$12.62	
15	Product Development Loading	20.0%	$2.52	$2.52	20.0%
16	Distribution Center Loading	5.0%	$0.63	$0.63	5.0%
17	In-Store		$15.78	$15.78	
18	Markup	75.0%	$21.03	$47.33	75.0%
19	Retail		$63.10	$63.10	
20	Markdown	35.0%	$22.09	$22.09	35.0%
21	Net Retail		$41.02	$41.02	
22	Net Retail Profit	40.0%	$25.24	$25.24	40.0%

Chapter 11
Reducing Markdowns

Markdown is the difference between the price on the hangtag and the average amount that the store receives after all sales and discounts. Markdowns occur for the simple reason that the goods do not sell. Some styles arrive at the store and sell out in a few days. Other styles don't sell at all. The blue and green sell but the red and the navy die. Sizes small and medium walk out of the store, while large and extra large just lay there.

There are three major causes of markdowns:

   a. Systemic: The factory is excluded from markdown reduction strategies.
   b. Structural: The business model adopted by brick and mortar stores requires markdowns.
   c. Unaccounted soft costs: Soft costs are important factors leading to markdowns. Their exclusion from garment costing precludes any ability to reduce markdowns.

Systemic Causes

Once again, this is to a large degree a costing problem. Because retailers and brands do not think of markdowns as a garment cost, markdowns do not appear on the cost sheet. They fail to recognize that not only are markdowns the single largest cost factor (more than twice total FOB), markdown costs can be substantially reduced by the factory. As we see in the cost sheet below, the markdown reduction on a garment with a $10.00 FOB price is $14.51 ($20.82 minus $6.31). It is as if rather than the customer paying the factory $10.00, the factory is paying the customer $4.51.

Markdowns are seldom the result of untalented designers or incompetent merchandisers. The main cause is time. If lead times for product development are six months and production and postproduction times add another five months, markdowns are inevitable. Who is so talented that they can predict what the consumer will want to buy a year in advance?

There are a number of strategies available to reduce markdowns but virtually all require SPEED-TO-MARKET. The most well-known strategy is Zara's strategy of DESIGN AFTER SALES. If the factory has FAST TURN capability with production lead times under seven days from FABRIC SPREADING to STOCK GOODS FINISHED, READY FOR SHIPMENT, it can follow the Zara model.

There are other benefits of speed-to-market:

- Trial orders: These are small quantities of multiple styles, produced and shipped by air in days. On receipt the retailer places the goods in pre-designated branch stores. If five styles sell well, the customer will place

The Guide to Cost-to-Value Analysis

bulk orders for those five styles. If three styles sell, the customer will place bulk orders for three styles. If zero styles sell, the customer will redesign and place new trial orders. Risk is minimized and money is saved.
- Quick response: When producing bulk orders, the factory retains a portion of the fabric for re-orders. Once the customer has detailed sales information from all stores, he is able to determine which styles, which colors and which sizes have the greatest sales and can place reorders with the knowledge that within six days the goods will be ready for air shipment.

Of course, fast turn capabilities require not only new skill sets but often a new factory layout. This is very costly both in time and capital but the returns are truly impressive. In our cost sheet below comparing costs when the factory does or does not offer markdown reduction services, **on the customer side, net profit (after markdowns) increases by $9.97 or 37.5%** ($26.50 to $36.47). **On the factory side net profit increases by 250%** (from $0.50 to $2.50 per unit).

		Full Value Costing: Factory With or Without Markdown (MD) Reduction Services			
			No Markdown Reduction	With Markdown Reduction	
			Cost	Cost	
1	Material		$6.00	$6.00	
2	Trim		$1.00	$1.00	
3	CM Labor		$0.64	$0.64	
4	CM Overhead		$1.86	$1.86	
5	Cost of Markdown Reduction Service		$0.00	$1.00	
6	CM Total Cost		$2.50	$3.50	
7	Total Factory Cost		$9.50	$10.50	
8	Added Value Markdown Reduction Service		$0.00	$2.00	
9	Net Factory Profit		$0.50	$2.50	
10	Total FOB Cost		$10.00	$13.00	
11	Agent Commission	5.0%	$0.50	$0.65	5.0%
12	Freight		$0.25	$0.25	
13	Duty (on Total FOB Cost)	16.2%	$1.62	$2.11	16.2%
14	Clearance		$0.10	$0.10	
15	Transport		$0.15	$0.15	
16	Total DDP		$12.62	$16.26	
17	Product Development Loading	20.0%	$2.52	$3.25	20.0%
18	Distribution Center Loading	5.0%	$0.63	$0.81	5.0%
19	In-Store		$15.78	$20.32	
20	Markup	75.0%	$47.33	$42.78	68.8%
21	Retail		$63.10	$63.10	
22	Markdown	33.0%	$20.82	$6.31	10.0%
23	Net Retail		$42.28	$56.79	
24	Net Customer Profit		$26.50	$36.47	$9.97

Chapter 11 Reducing Markdowns

- Line 5: Assumes factory MD reduction services cost of $1.00 per unit.
- Line 6: CM without MD reduction services $2.50. With is $3.50.
- Line 8: Factory added profit for providing MD reduction services is $2.00.
- Line 9: Total factory profit including MD reduction services $2.50. Without is 50¢.
- Line 10: FOB cost including MD reduction services $13.00. Without is $10.00.
- Line 16: DDP cost including MD reduction services $16.26. Without is $12.62.
- Line 17: Product Development where factory provides service = $3.25. Where customer charges PD loading = $2.52[1]
- Line 19: Cost in-store where factory provides MD reduction services is $20.32. Without is $15.78.
- Line 21: Retail price for both cases is the same = $63.10.
Markup where factory provides MD reduction services is 69%.
Markup where factory does not is 75%.
- Line 22: When factory helps reduce MDs, it can drop to 10% of retail or $6.31. Otherwise MD stays at 33% or $20.82.
- Line 24: Retail net profit where factory provides MD reduction services is $36.47. Without the factory services, retail net profit is $26.50.
- Customer's net savings when factory helps reduce MDs is $9.97.

Structural Causes

Fashion garment retail has only two basic models:

- Selling something to everybody
- Selling something to somebody

Today brick and mortar retail follows the something-for-everybody model. It is simply a question of geography. The retail store by definition has a fixed location. Its potential customer base is limited to the distance a customer will travel to get to the store. A customer might travel 50 miles but not 500 miles.

Success is based entirely on increased market share, the ability to draw the potential customer away from other brick and mortar competitors. To maximize its customer base, the store must sell fashion that appeals to the greatest number of potential customers and at prices that will further attract those customers.

But reality is different: the something-for-everybody model defined as fashion-for-everybody strategy has put the major retailers in a hole for two reasons:

---

1   The importer customer does not know the actual product development costs and for good reason. Instead they will use a loading, a percentage added to the cost of every imported garment, usually about 20% of DDP.

The Guide to Cost-to-Value Analysis

- To succeed the retailer must reduce design to the lowest common denominator because the more individualized the design, the smaller the potential customer base;
- To succeed the retailer must have sufficient stock of every style, in every color and every size to meet potential consumer demand. The retailer cannot afford to sell out of any style because every lost sale reduces market share.

In this regard, markdowns are not evidence of a failure of design, merchandising or sourcing skills, but rather the necessary result of the never-ending fight for lower costs. This in turn limits the ability of the designers to create the best designs, the sourcing specialists to work with the best factories and the merchandising executives to select the best style rather those with the lowest cost.

Markdowns will continue to grow, resulting in ever-increasing retail prices until brick-and-mortar retailers change their business model or are replaced by other retailers with a more rational business model.

Unaccounted Soft Cost Causes

Soft costs come in two distinct types but have one thing in common: We can quantify the added cost but not the added value. Positive soft costs such as quality and design come with cost. Higher quality and better design will invariably add cost which is quantifiable. At the same time, these added costs will be more than offset by higher value, which is not quantifiable.

If we look back, the data is clear. As we saw in the Gap case study, under Drexler when high quality was a primary goal, the company reached its peak in 2005 with sales of $16.3bn and profits of $1.2bn (7.1% of volume). In the post-Drexler era, when quality was sacrificed in order to reduce costs, the company declined. For 2018, sales totaled $15.9bn with profits of $848mn (5.3% of volume).

Negative soft costs pose even greater problems. For example, greater compliance, sustainability and transparency all come with added cost but those costs are difficult to calculate because they are offset by other factors. A factory operating with high level corporate social responsibility (CSR) may be able to attract better quality customers who demand high levels of CSR from the suppliers. In this case, the added cost of CSR could be offset by the increase in value they provide to their customer who is willing to pay a higher FOB price.

The difficulty comes at the consumer level. The consumer may require greater compliance, sustainability and transparency, but they will not buy just because the retailer and brand has good CSR. That same consumer may well reject retailers and brands with low levels of CSR.

We live in a world where the consumer is looking for reasons not-to-buy. Today

Chapter 11 Reducing Markdowns

a consumer looking for a blue wool overcoat need only input that request on their computer and 800+ pictures will immediately pop up. No one wants to go through 800 photographs before deciding on their overcoat of choice. It is much easier to narrow down the selection by blocking whole groups. The consumer can easily find lists compiled by NGOs for factories which are deemed unsustainable or who allegedly mistreat their workers. Put in the names and let the computer do the work. Searching for the so-called good CSR factories is also easy. Ethical behavior becomes a game allowing the consumer a double benefit. Not only can they pat themselves on the back for their ethical behavior, they also reduce the time spent surfing the endless choices available on the internet.

Chapter 12
The Competitive Model

This is where the industry began. In the 1950s, at the outset of overseas garment buying, both the customer and his factory supplier had minimal skill sets and products were limited to basic low-quality commodities: t-shirts, cotton casual pants, basic woven cotton shirts and underwear. If the factory's product was a men's woven shirt to retail for 99¢, low FOB price was everything.

Today, over six decades later, many retailers, particularly those in the mass-market sector, still follow the competitive model, as do their factory suppliers and even the national industries where they work including Bangladesh, Pakistan, Cambodia and most of the CAFTA-DR countries. The competitive model is alive and well, with successful companies on both sides.

Over time, the customer has developed new tools to reduce FOB prices. We have already discussed how negotiations over prices have evolved as the industry went from GARMENT BUYING to GARMENT SOURCING and now finally to OPEN SOURCING. With each era, the customer's sourcing specialist, with the assistance of new technology, is increasingly able to determine and dictate the exact prices of all materials and labor minutes required for each style (bearing in mind differences in productivity from one region to another). Today's sourcing specialist no longer negotiates prices on a style by style basis. Instead the only remaining negotiations revolve around how much the customer is willing to pay per minute for all production, regardless of the style.

Case Study X: Sam Schmata's Re-re-education

Sam has been running his factory for a very long time. He fondly remembers the days when Arnie the Goniff was buyer. "Arnie would show up with the sample. I would quote an FOB price. Arnie would reject the price. I would quote a second, third, fifteenth FOB price until it was time for him to a catch the plane to go home to Brooklyn, at which point we would agree on the price we knew from Day 1 was going to be the agreed price. Arnie the Goniff was not what you would call a nice man, but at least I understood him."

Everything went okay until the day Wendell Wasp, the 25-year-old kid, showed up. "Where's Arnie the buyer?" Sam asks.

"Forget about the Goniff. He's out. I'm in and everything is changed", Wendell answers.
"Step 1: I do not want to hear about your FOB price. FOB is out. CM is in.
"Step 2: Here is the price I negotiated with the textile mill and this is what you are going to pay for fabric.
"Step 3: Here is the trim sheet, with the names of all the designated trim suppliers and their prices and that is what you are going to pay for trim.
"Step 4: All I care about is CM. Your labor cost, your overhead, your profit – if any."

Welcome to the world of garment sourcing!

The Guide to Cost-to-Value Analysis

> Things change. Sam gets used to it. And just when he finally figures out how to make a profit, last week in walks John Von Neumann in his double-breasted blazer, white shirt and ascot. "So where is Wendell Wasp, the sourcing man?" Sam asks.
>
> "Forget about Mr. Wasp, crude man that he was. I am surprised that you were able to put up with him all those years. This is the new open sourcing era, and you and I are going to get along swimmingly. No conflicts. No stress. No arguments," says John.
>
> "This is how we will work. Let's take our blouse style 1462S. We know the fabric cost is $3.39. We calculate consumption, naturally including damage and wastage, so 2.365mts. (If you have some problem with consumption, we can provide the markers). Trim, according to the trim sheet, equals $1.16.
>
> "All that is left is CM. Based on our research we have determined that factories in your area should operate at 75% productivity so style 1462S should require 30 minutes production time. We are generously giving you 40 minutes. We think 6¢ per minute is fair, which means we will pay you $2.40 CM. Oh yes, you will need 16¢ to pay for local transport", John rattles on.
>
> "So FOB price for style 1462S is $11.74. What the hell, let's call it $11.75. After all, we are friends. And here are the price breakdowns for the 37 styles we have scheduled for you for the next six months.
>
> "I told you. Things are easy now. No conflicts. No stress. No arguments. If you have any problems, do not hesitate to contact me, but I would be really grateful that you go along with me, unless of course you find a serious error, which frankly I doubt.
>
> "You and I are going to have a great time together. See you in six months."
>
> This is progress???

Let's look at what happens during the traditional competitive one-sided negotiations where the customer dictated prices. The table below shows what happens if the customer arbitrarily decides that they only want to pay $9.50 FOB instead of the $10.00 which the factory is hoping for with a 5% profit on their costs. The table below shows that the customer eventually saves 60cts per item by the time the item lands in their country while the factory makes zero profits.

Chapter 12 The Competitive Model

		Customer Reduces FOB Price From $10.00 to $9.50			
			$10.00 FOB	$9.50 FOB	
		Factors	Cost	Price	
1	Material		$6.00	$6.00	
2	Trim		$1.00	$1.00	
3	CM Labor		$0.64	$0.64	
4	CM Overhead*		$1.86	$1.86	
5	CM Total Cost		$2.50	$2.50	
6	Added Costs				
7	Total Cost		$9.50	$9.50	
8	Added Profit			-$0.50	
9	Factory Profit		$0.50	$0.00	
10	Total FOB Cost		$10.00	$9.50	
11	Agent Commission	5.0%	$0.50	$0.48	5.0%
12	Freight		$0.25	$0.25	
13	Duty	16.2%	$1.62	$1.54	16.2%
14	Clearance		$0.10	$0.10	
15	Transport		$0.15	$0.15	
16	Total DDP		$12.62	$12.02	
		Customer Savings		$0.60	

*CM Overhead calculated at 2.9 times CM Labor as per industry standard

Now let's look at what happens under open sourcing, the latest iteration of the traditional customer controls all price negotiations. Here the customer announces they will pay 6cts per minute even though the factory can show it needs 7.5cts per minute in order to make 5% profit. Since the labor and overhead is fixed, the difference of 60¢ must come from the factory's profit, reducing its anticipated profit of 50¢ (5% of FOB) to a loss of 10¢ (-1.1% of FOB) while the customer's savings now increases to 73cts.

The Guide to Cost-to-Value Analysis

		40 Minute Garment Before and After Open Sourcing @ 6¢ per Minute				
			No Open Sourcing		With Open Sourcing	
		Factors	Cost	Price	Factors	
1	Fabric		$6.00	$6.00		
2	Trim		$1.00	$1.00		
3	CM Labor		$0.64	$0.64		
4	CM Overhead		$1.86	$1.86		
5	CM Total Cost		$2.50	$2.50		
6	CM Price (incl Profit)	7.5¢	$3.00	$2.40	6¢	
7	Total Cost		$9.50	$9.40		
8	FOB Price		$10.00	$9.40		
9	Factory Profit	5.0%	$0.50	-$0.10	-1.1%	
10	Agent Commission	5%	$0.50	$0.47		
11	Freight		$0.25	$0.25		
12	Duty	16.2%	$1.62	$1.52		
13	Clearance		$0.10	$0.10		
14	Transport		$0.15	$0.15		
15	Total DDP		$12.62	$11.89		
16	Product Development Loading	20%	$2.52	$2.52		
17	Distribution Center Loading	5%	$0.63	$0.63		
18	In-Store		$15.78	$15.04		
19	Markup	75%	$47.33	$45.13		
20	Retail		$63.11	$63.11		
21	Gross Profit		$47.34	$48.07		
22	Markdown	35%	$22.09	$22.09		
23	Net Retail		$41.02	$41.02		
24	Net Customer Profit		$25.25	$25.98	$0.73	

To the customer, open sourcing is very good as a negotiating strategy. A large importer, placing 5000+ orders per month in 1000+ factories located in 10 countries, may have 100 factories supplying woven shirts. With open sourcing, the importer no longer has the burden of negotiating every order with every supplier. At the same time, the importer is able to compare FOB prices simultaneously with every factory in every country. For the first time, the customer is able to receive real answers in real time.

The problem is that at 6¢ per minute the factory, as we have seen in the cost sheet above, shows a loss. To the importer following the competitive model, this is not a problem. These are zero-service factories whose role is simply production. There are many factories whose capabilities are limited to producing a decent garment, on time, and at a competitive price. Any factory that cannot meet the customer's target price is easily replaceable.

Chapter 13
The Cooperative Model

As a tool for gathering data for the customer, open sourcing is exceptional. But as a way of negotiating FOB prices, it is not particularly good because the winning factory will be zero-service, capable of providing nothing but low CM.

Furthermore, the total cost saving of $0.73 is just over 1% of the customer's $63.11 retail price. More knowledgeable customers and suppliers have recognized that perhaps greater savings would be possible if they considered the other 99%. The arrival of full-value costing finally permitted both the customer and the supplier to quantify both the added costs and value.

There was an underlying problem. The goal was for the factory to provide value-added services which will lead to added profit for its customer in the form of cost reduction and to the factory in the form of higher profit. But the supplier very often did not have the skill sets necessary to carry out those value-added services. Over time the customer and the supplier, working together, arrived at solutions whereby the customer would work directly with important suppliers to develop these services. Today, many customers have specialty departments including engineers and other professionals for the specific purpose of upgrading factory skill sets. This is the essence of the cooperative model.

The table below shows what happens when product development is transferred from the customer to the factory and how each side benefits.

		Product Development Cost Comparison			
		Customer Provides Product Development		Factory Provides Product Development	
		Factors	Cost	Cost	Factors
1	Material		$6.00	$6.00	
2	Trim		$1.00	$1.00	
3	CM Labor		$0.64	$0.64	
4	CM Overhead		$1.86	$1.86	
5	Cost of Service Product Development		$0.00	$0.25	
6	CM Total Cost		$2.50	$2.75	
7	Total Factory Cost		$9.50	$9.75	
8	Added Factory Cost PD		$0.00	$0.25	
9	Net Factory Profit	5.0%	$0.50	$0.75	7.5%
10	Total FOB Cost		$10.00	$10.50	
11	Agent Commission	5.0%	$0.50	$0.53	5.0%
12	Freight		$0.25	$0.25	
13	Duty	16.2%	$1.62	$1.70	16.2%

The Guide to Cost-to-Value Analysis

14	Clearance			$0.10	$0.10	
15	Local Transport			$0.15	$0.15	
16	Total LDP			$12.62	$13.23	
17	Product Development Loading	20.0%		$2.52	$0.26	2.0%
18	Distribution Center Loading	2.5%		$0.32	$0.33	2.5%
19	Total Cost In-Store			$15.46	$13.82	
20	Markup	75.0%		$46.38	$48.02	77.7%
21	Retail Price			$61.84	$61.84	
22	Markdown	35.0%		$21.64	$21.64	35.0%
23	Net Retail			$40.19	$40.19	
24	Net Retail Profit (After Markdown)			$24.73	$26.37	**$1.64**

- Line 5: Assumes factory per unit cost of PD: 25¢
- Line 6: CM without PD is $2.50. CM with PD is $2.75.
- Line 8: Factory added profit for PD: 25¢
- Line 9: Total factory profit including PD: 75¢. Without PD: 50¢.
- Line 10: FOB cost including PD at factory is $10.50. Without PD: $10.00.
- Line 16: DDP cost including PD at factory $13.23. Without PD: $12.62.
- Line 17: Additional PD work in home country when factory provides service: 26¢
  Where customer carries out entire PD service and charges a loading = $2.52[1]
- Line 19: Cost in-store where factory provides PD = $13.82.
  Where customer carries out PD = $15.46.
- Line 21: Retail price for both is the same = $61.84[2]:
  Markup when factory provides PD = 78%
  Markup when customer provides PD = 75%
- Line 24: Retail net profit where factory provides PD ($40.19 - $13.82) = $26.37
  Retail net profit where customer provides PD ($40.19 - $15.46) = $24.73
- Customer's net savings when factory provides PD = $1.64
  Factory's increased profit when providing PD = 25¢ (50¢ to 75¢)

Moving product development from the customer to the factory results in substantial increased benefit for both the customer and his supplier. The customer, now cooperating with the factory, sees his savings more than doubled to $1.64 from the $0.60 or $0.73 cost sheet savings that we've looked at under the competitive model in the previous chapter.

---

1 Once again, the importer customer does not know the actual product development costs and instead adds a percentage loading, 20% of DDP for our purposes.
2 We assume the retailer retains the cost savings in the form of added profit, with the result that the retail price remains unchanged.

Chapter 13 The Cooperative Model

Furthermore, the customer receives two other more important benefits:

- Guaranteed QA: Since the factory carries out the product development, the customer can be assured that the factory can produce stock of the same quality;
- Design Integrity: As we discussed before, all too often the sample does not follow the designer's sketch and the stock does not follow the sample. When, however, the entire process is in the hands of the factory, under the designer's supervision, the customer can rest assured knowing that the integrity of the style has been maintained throughout.

On the factory side, net profit increases a substantial 50% from $0.50 to $0.75 per unit. Last but not least, the factory's relationship with its customer is solidified because of the added value it provides.

If we combine all the data that we've arrived at in our various comparative cost sheets, we get the following table. Except for the loss to the factory whose customer is using open sourcing but who considers the factory to be zero-service, moving up the ladder and offering more services gives quantifiable increased benefit for both customer and factory.

	Customer	Factory
Traditional Model	Savings $0	Profit $0.50
Competitive Model	Savings $0.60 - $0.73	Profit 0¢
Cooperative Model: Product Development	Savings $1.64	Profit $0.75

But when we look at the benefits achievable with reduced markdowns, those savings for the customer can be increased by as much as six times and profits to the factory increased by a still impressive three times.

	Customer	Factory
Traditional Model	Savings $0	Profit $0.50
Cooperative Model: Product Development	Savings $1.64	Profit $0.75
Cooperative Model: Reduced Markdown	Savings $9.97	Profit $2.50

BOOK II
Where Do You Want to Go and How Do You Get There

Chapter 14
The Collaborative Model: Part I

The collaborative model is different. The previous competitive and cooperative models were all about cost reduction. The collaborative model is all about doing things that previously have not been possible. Even this definition fails to explain how this new model differs from everything that has come before. Let's try again. The previous models were created by the industry. This new collaborative model is the result of outside events that have been thrust on the industry that will change the industry forever.

The move from the competitive to the cooperative model did not take place uniformly. There are still plenty of major customers and entire national garment-exporting industries that are attached to the old competitive model. Both sides have plenty of complaints. Customers argue that if their suppliers would do more, they, the customers, would pay more, while their suppliers complain that they would do more if only their customers would pay more.

Other customers belong to the IF-BUT BRIGADE. Yes, they argue, value-added services are important, and we would welcome them – if these services did not result in higher FOB prices. This group stands by the belief that it doesn't matter how much profit the factory makes. IT MATTERS ONLY HOW MUCH PROFIT THE CUSTOMER MAKES.

Enter the collaborative model with new players from outside the industry.

Rise of the Buyers' Market

Traditionally the industry supply chain consisted of two parties: the customer (retailer and brand) and the supplier (factory). In this two-part relationship, the customer was king. The role of the supplier was to carry out the customer's instructions. This was the competitive model where the consumer played a passive role in the supply chain. The customer decided what the consumer wanted, had the supplier make it, and then sold it to the consumer.

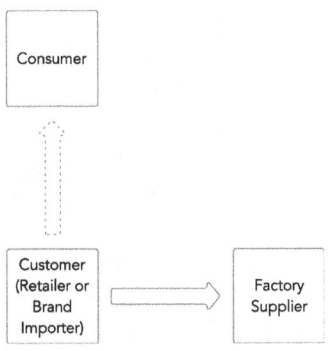

The Guide to Cost-to-Value Analysis

This is how every consumer goods industry, from automobiles to clothing, operated. While it was undeniably true that from time to time the consumer would not buy what the customer was selling, this was thought to be the result of temporary external economic conditions such as recession. Consumers were not buying General Motor cars because they were not buying cars, period. GM would reduce costs by laying off workers with the certain knowledge that when the recession ended, sales would pick up, laid-off workers would return to work and profits would increase again.

Nothing changed until 1 June 2009 when GM went broke and management saw that consumers were still buying cars, just not GM cars. To put it another way, the problem was not external, that CONSUMERS WERE NOT BUYING WHAT GM WAS SELLING, but rather internal, that GM WAS NOT SELLING WHAT CONSUMERS WERE BUYING.

Professionals talk about a consumer-driven market as something unusual that occurs from time to time. The reality is that the true consumer-driven market is quite rare, the last true one occurring in Florence in 1425. The next time you visit Florence, go to the Santa Maria Novella church. See the Masaccio fresco of the Holy Trinity, which shows Jesus, St. John, the Virgin Mary, and the Holy Ghost together with a guy and his wife named Lenzi. Who was Lenzi? Lenzi is the guy who paid for the painting. IT'S MY MONEY, MY PAINTING, MY WIFE AND I ARE INCLUDED IN THE HOLY TRINITY. Welcome to the great consumer-driven market.

Today's consumers, led by the millennials, are just as powerful as Mr. and Mrs. Lenzi, only their power is more nuanced. Most consumers buying garments want the same things – interesting design, good fit, good make and the right price.

Chapter 14 The Collaborative Model: Part I

At the same time, there is a minority, perhaps 10% of all consumers, who want that and more. They add:

- Compliance: They do not want the clothing on their backs made by ten-year-old children working 70-hour weeks.
- Sustainability: They do not want the factory taking ground water, mixing it with toxic chemicals and pushing it back into the ground.
- Transparency: They want proof that the product is made in a place that operates in compliance with good labor practices and is sustainable.

It is that 10% that controls the direction the industry must now follow.

We operate in a segmented market where different people expect different things. The vast majority of consumers may have little or no interest in those things, but to the consumers who care, those things determine where they will *not* buy. As we have already seen, when we consider child labor, the difference is not between those who are anti-child-labor and those who are pro-child-labor. Nobody is pro-child-labor. For the retailer planning to remain in business, there is no choice, child labor is *verboten*.

But for the smart retailer who wishes to meet the demands of the 10%, the way forward is not easy. Some retailers are indeed moving ahead joining organizations committed to greater corporate responsibility. They have come together to form groups such as the Alliance in Bangladesh that are committed to improving working conditions in local factories. Some are developing creative solutions, such as the circular supply chain where retailers take back old worn-out clothing, which they then break down to create new products such as building insulation. These are important developments.

But the 10% are guided by special attributes not the least of which we will call *informed cynicism*. We live in world where the new generation of consumers have dumped senior managers of major brands and retailers as well as factory suppliers into the same circle of hell as politicians and pederasts. In this new market, advertising counts for less than nothing. It has been overtaken by social media where ordinary people review and critique every product from marijuana to tampons.

Retailers simply cannot sell to these people. They cannot market nor advertise the quality or price of their goods. In fact any attempt to sell will result in a negative reaction whereby the consumer will simply refuse to buy. The retailer/brand customer can only rely on their ability to meet the requirements of the 10% but the 10% are exceedingly tough. The customer operates in a one-strike-you're-out environment. A single incident of poor compliance or unsustainable activity on their part or on the part of one of their suppliers is immediately posted on social media putting the brand and/or retailer in deep trouble.

The supplier side is in better shape. The demands of the 10%, particularly with regard to transparency, puts them in a position to prove their reliability because the factory has direct control of its compliance and sustainability.

The Guide to Cost-to-Value Analysis

The Advent of the Small E-Commerce Retailer

Case Study XI: A Short History of Retail

1.

   | Brick & Mortar Retailer |

   In the beginning, before the advent of the global garment export/import industry, all retail was carried out by brick & mortar (B&M) stores.

2.

   | Brick & Mortar Retailer | ← | Brand |

   In the early days the garments were designed by the brands who produced the garments in domestic factories and in turn wholesaled the goods to the B&M stores.

3.

   | Private Label | → | Brick & Mortar Retailer | ← | Brand |

   In the 1970s the B&M stores decided that rather than pay the brands a substantial markup, they would move into private label. Instead of buying from the brands, the stores created their own brands and produced the goods themselves.

4.

   | Brand | → | Brand B&M Store |

   Just as the stores cut out the brands to avoid paying the added markup, the brands began to open their own B&M stores.

5. Advent of SME e-commerce: From Consumer to Competitor

   | SME E-Commerce |

   E-commerce has changed forever the face of garment retail. All the impediments to opening retail operations have disappeared. Advantages of e-commerce operations include:

   a. Small capital requirements
      i. No investment in building, furniture and fixtures
      ii. Little or no staff
      iii. Little or no advertising and promotion
   b. Smaller inventory
      i. Fewer styles
      ii. Smaller quantities
   c. Expanding from local market to global market
   d. Individualized niche products

   In the new e-commerce market all that is needed is a good idea and good business sense.

Chapter 14 The Collaborative Model: Part I

6. The New Model Industry: Everybody does Everything

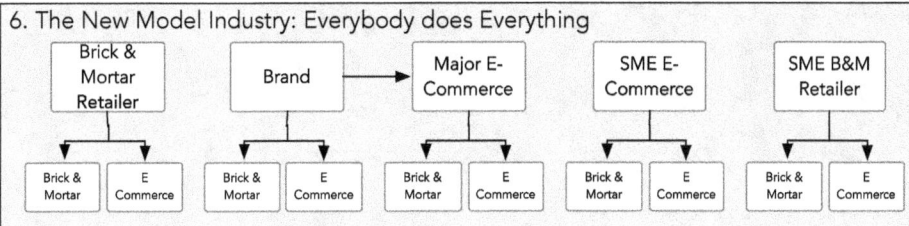

The advent of the internet has brought fundamental change. The old sector definitions no longer exist.
- There is no longer any division between B&M stores and e-commerce. Today virtually all B&M retailers are into e-commerce, while e-commerce retailers are increasingly opening B&M operations.
- The division between wholesalers and retailers are gone. Brands that previously wholesaled their products to retailers have both opened their own stores and sold their products either through their own e-commerce operation and/or via Amazon and other major e-commerce operations.
- The concept of a separate private label sector is disappearing. Today companies that previously saw their future as private label producers for B&M retailers are now moving to work directly with the consumer, again either through their own e-commerce operations or through the major e-commerce companies.

Once again it is the customer side that faces the problems. They must reinvent themselves if they are to meet the needs of the consumer. On the other hand, the factory supplier side enjoys great opportunities because the world will always need garments.

There are three requirements for customers and suppliers to work under the collaborative model:

1. Both sides must benefit from the partnership. The benefit might not be shared equally but it must be real and quantifiable.
2. Both sides must offer open data. Any attempt to hide data or worse, to distort the data, will result in failure of the partnership.
3. Each side must be responsible. Real success goes to the truly talented on both sides.

The collaborative model, which currently has few if any followers, will change the industry forever.

Chapter 15
Technology I: From Analogue to Digital

An analogue is something parallel or comparable to something else. It is not the thing itself. The traditional watch, the sextant and the early computers are all analogues. The traditional clock consists two or three hands that rotate within a circle. By locating the position of each hand within the circle, we can determine the time. The digital version is an object which actually shows the time, for example, 10:43.31.

A sextant is a device that measures the angle of the sun to the horizon which together with an accurate clock will allow a sailor to determine the latitude location of the ship during daylight hours while at sea. The digital version is GPS, a box connected to a satellite that gives the location of a person or a vehicle, anywhere and anytime. The early computers provided data in binary code, a series of 0s and 1s, which the user had to translate into usable data. The modern digital version provides data and written material directly onto the screen.

The move from analogue to digital has solved many of the inaccuracies and problems which the garment industry has faced since it moved from bespoke to mass-produced products.

The first problem is garment size: S-M-L, 6-16, 46-56. Size is in fact based on three measurements:

   a. Shape: a person's actual body measurements from which fit is derived
   b. Fit: the garment measurements based on shape from which size is derived
   c. Size: an alphanumerical character based on fit which allows the consumer to select the garment that correctly coincides with their body

These analogues are translated into the patterns, grading and markers necessary to physically cut the fabric into garment parts. From the dawn of the industry, garment professionals have been aware of the many serious shortcomings with the analogue-based sizing system:

   a. Every person has his or her unique shape, yet the entire sizing system worldwide including men, women, boys, girls and infants has an aggregate of perhaps 200 sizes. That means that in a world of 7.5 billion people where each person's shape is unique, each person is shoehorned into a category of 37,500,000 people.
   b. Size differs with each brand. A size 10 at Ralph Lauren may be a size 8 at Target.

The Guide to Cost-to-Value Analysis

    c. Size between countries differ. A size 12 in the UK is approximately equivalent to a size 10 in the U.S., while size 36 differs between Germany, France and Italy.

The second problem occurs when the factory is called upon to translate size into a pattern required to cut the fabric into garment parts.

    a. A pattern is a two-dimensional object used to produce a three-dimensional garment. By its very nature, the pattern is a poor representation of fit and shape.

    b. The pattern must take into consideration the fabric, for example, its drape. Two identical styles each utilizing a different fabric will require two separate sets of patterns. Where a fabric has a very soft drape, such as georgette or fine gauge single jersey, it becomes virtually impossible to create a pattern from the designer's sketch. In some cases, even the same fabric in different colors will have different drapes and require different patterns. In these instances patternmakers must cut the actual fabric into approximate pattern pieces, put the pieces together on a mannequin; see the degree the resulting sample is incorrect; recut the fabric to make the necessary corrections and repeat the process over and over until the final basted sample reflects the correct design.

A third problem is the transition from single pattern to the graded set. The difference between one size to another, as measured in centimeters, is not fixed. For example, the difference between size 4 to size 6 is less than the difference between size 10 to size 12, which in turn is less than between size 16 to size 18. At the same time grading based on 5-10 measurements – dress = chest, waist, hips, length, shoulder, cross back, etc. – will not provide good fit. At the end of the day grading is a highly developed craft.

Today, as technology moves us from analogue to digital, we have new techniques.

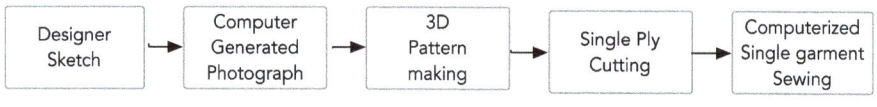

We can now translate a designer sketch into a computer-generated photograph showing a model wearing the finished garment – in the correct fabric – allowing for the correct drape.

- From which the computer can take the photograph to generate a three-dimensional pattern;
- From which a single-ply cutter can provide the required garment parts;
- From which a computerized sewing machine can produce a single sample.

Chapter 15 Technology I: From Analogue to Digital

The same system can be adapted for bulk garment production, conceivably up to and including in-store delivery. Lead time from receipt of confirmed order broken down by size/style/wash to arrival of finished garments at each branch store can be as fast as 20 days.

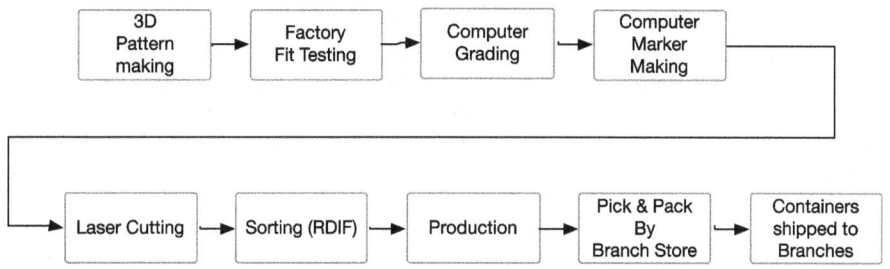

The move from analogue to digital has created other advances beginning with the problem of fit.

1. Databases are now available to define shape for thousands of consumers in different countries, therefore permitting fit to relate more closely to shape.
2. Databases exist to allow consumers to relate size from one brand to another; e.g., if you are size 10 at Marks & Spencer, the computer will tell you your size at Gap, Hilfiger, Primark or H&M.
3. Computer systems currently exist to scan the individual to provide an eight-digit size that can be transferred to the factory's grading system allowing for virtual customization.

Blockchain Technology

Traditionally if a retailer/brand wanted to trace the upstream materials that went into their products such as fabric, yarn and fiber, they had little choice. Either they worked with a vertically integrated supplier that carried out all manufacturing in-house or they went to the old reliable method of BOOT-ON-GROUND, dispatching people to check each production stage, including, in the case of cotton, into the field where it is grown. Blockchain changed everything by providing a third more reliable and less expensive alternative.

A blockchain is a growing list of records, called blocks, that are linked using cryptography. Each block contains a code of the previous block. Material can be entered but once entered cannot be altered. Together this forms a series of transactions, which allows the user to trace the steps in a supply chain. In 2016 Target used blockchain technology to trace the steps in various supply chains with unforeseen results.

The Guide to Cost-to-Value Analysis

> Case Study XII: Welspun and Egyptian Cotton Bedlinen
>
> For many years Target enjoyed a successful business selling bedlinen to their consumers. The quality was good, the prices competitive, and the sheets and pillowcases were made of Egyptian long-staple cotton.
>
> All went well until in 2016, Target began to employ blockchain technology to analyze upstream materials and discovered that the yarn produced by its major supplier Welspun India Ltd (WIL) was not of Egyptian origin. On 19 August 2016, Target notified all their customers who had purchased this bedlinen, ordering a recall and offering refunds, and of course severed all ties with WIL.
>
> Target's use of blockchain together with their culture of total transparency allowed the company to get in front of the problem without any loss of reputation. Consider what would have resulted otherwise. The situation would have continued unabated with WIL shipping faux-Egyptian cotton yarn until some doctoral student at North Carolina State University decided to write his thesis on DNA testing of percale yarns. The thesis would have been published and the student praised for his fine investigative work. Then given the litigious nature of U.S. society, a very large and drawn-out class action suit would have followed.
>
> The loss of reputation aside, the estimated direct costs of such a class action suit would easily be several hundred millions of dollars. This is but a simple example of how value-added services can be quantified.

Mass Customization

Today, when we talk of mass customization, there are currently two separate strategies. Both are included in the collaborative model because both require a partnership between the customer (importer, retailer and/or brand) and the supplier (factory). In some cases, the collaborative model relationship occurs when the customer and supplier become one-and-the-same, for example, when factories open their own retail or e-commerce outlets, or the two recognize that one cannot exist without the other.

Small mass customization is when the consumer can buy custom made suits, jeans, or shirts made exactly to his size using 3D fitting, 3D patternmaking, single-ply computerized cutting and single-piece robotic sewing. A customer for such services would likely have previously purchased bespoke jeans at Barney's for anywhere from $800-$1500.

Big mass customization is where the factory can provide:
- 1 million jeans
- In 1000 sizes
- In 14 days
- At no increased price.

Chapter 15 Technology I: From Analogue to Digital

The consumer goes into a Walmart equipped with 3D fitting machines. Gone are the S-M-L-XL-XXL sizes. The consumer is given an eight-digit number for his size. To ensure that his jeans will be the right fit, Walmart staff are constantly following up previous orders of customized product.

The consumer chooses one of three models, each available in three washes meaning there are a total of nine possibilities. The factory receives the individual orders in real time. The computer generates the size breakdown for all individualized sizes per style at the same time but each cutting will only include 12 sizes based on the maximum size of the marker. Each cutting will therefore include the 12 greatest selling sizes. As new sales figures come into the computer, new markers are generated based on the greatest selling sizes and the date of order receipt.

Assuming the factory has 20 tables each cutting four times a day: 48,000 pieces could be cut in a day and one million pieces in a 20-day month. Given Walmart's scale, sales of 48,000 pieces a day is quite conservative. Bear in mind there is no total order size. Sales come in every day for each model/wash permutation available.

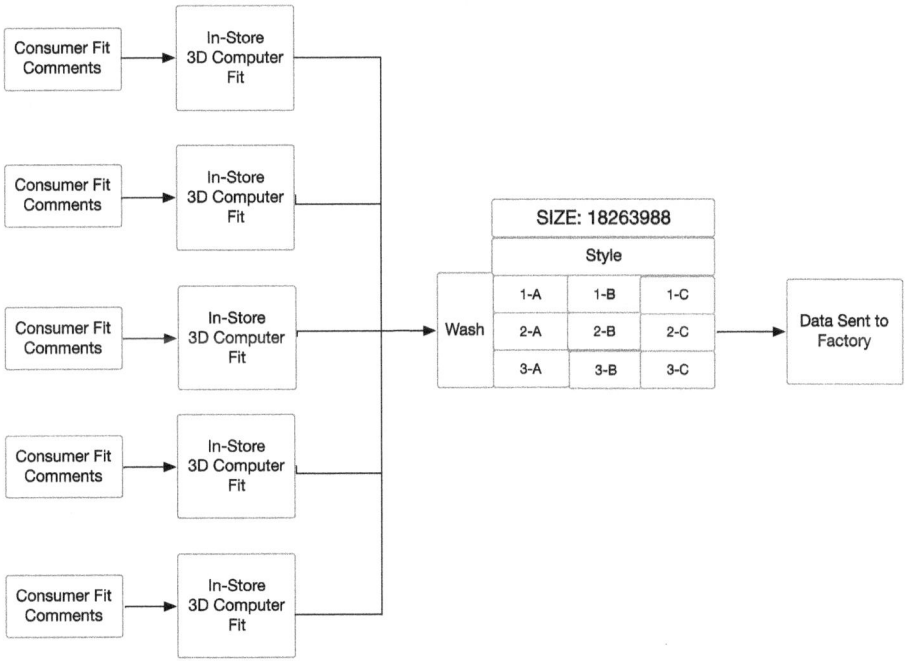

The move from analogue to digital customization is still in its nascent form. It is too early to determine where this will lead and which system will become the industry standard.

Chapter 16
Technology II: Soft Technology Alternatives

Our industry is in the midst of a technological revolution. This presents two serious problems: Where is it taking us? Do we want to go there?

We have been brought up to believe that we are in the midst of a second industrial revolution when once again workers will be replaced with more productive machines. It is true that the first industrial revolution was based on textile machinery such as the Spinning Jenny, the Flying Shuttle and Crompton's Spinning Mule which were indeed not only more efficient and more cost-effective but also produced a higher quality product than handmade goods.

However, what was true in the 18th century is not true today. We might think it is true only if we assume that industry operates best when workers have been turned into machines and if that is true, then it follows that the machine must be better than the worker. But there is another way to look at things. Technology works best when it is not the driving force but rather the tool of an educated and well-trained worker. Technology has brought many advances to the garment industry and in future will certainly bring many more.

It is possible that within our lifetime Artificial Intelligence will be able to predict what styles consumers want. At that point brands and retailers need no longer take enormous risks producing goods that consumers will not buy. This in turn will markedly reduce markdowns that have plagued our industry.

It is possible that within our lifetime, computer-driven machinery together with sophisticated software will reduce product development from six+ months to two to three days. It is possible that through very sophisticated software, computers will be able to create true 3D patterns that will mirror shape and fit. It is possible that eventually computerized machinery and sophisticated software will allow factories to increase productivity, replace workers, and finally put an end to wage inflation.

We are not by any means there yet, but based on the latest advances, the technology that only a few years ago would have been considered impossible has now become a certainty – at some point in the future. All that is required is time, effort and money. Which leaves us with but one question: Why bother?

I am quite serious. Why are we trying to predict what consumers want to buy when 40 years ago Inditex developed a foolproof six-step method to do a near perfect job? Zara literally designs after sales! They operate under trial orders which works like this:

The Guide to Cost-to-Value Analysis

1. Take one factory with speed-to-market capability.
2. Produce limited quantities of multiple styles.
3. Ship the trial orders to designated target stores.
4. Wait five days.
5. Determine which styles sell and which do not sell.
6. Order bulk production of the bestseller styles.

Why are we trying to invent complex and costly computerized hardware and sophisticated software to reduce product development lead times when 40 years ago the same Inditex developed another foolproof six-step method? Zara carries out most of the product development work before there is even a product to develop.

1. Go on a computer. All new fashion exists on the internet – shows, store windows, etc.
2. Download the most interesting designs.
3. Produce patterns and knit specs for all downloaded designs.
4. Select the best designs for the particular fabric.
5. Wait for the sample fabric to arrive.
6. Produce the sample in two to three days.

Why are we investing large sums in the hope that expensive machinery will improve productivity when in most of the garment-producing countries even the best and most efficient machines are not cost-effective? Even in the industrialized high-labor rate countries, computerized machinery is at best an important tool for well-educated, highly trained workers.

For many years, the best factory executives have recognized that worker training provides the best and by far the most cost-effective method to increase productivity. The data and results are so clear that we must assume that factories and national industries that fail to rely on worker training must have priorities other than success and added profit.

There is one possibility that might explain both the success of worker training and the failure of some to move in that direction. All worker training whether it be teams, lean manufacturing or modular systems, depend on worker empowerment. Cultures that fear worker empowerment will not accept worker training as a means of increasing productivity even if it means the factory will not increase profits.

The problem is that while engineers can provide the necessary training, they cannot create worker empowerment. For this we have to look to SOFT TECHNOLOGY.

Chapter 16   Technology II: Soft Technology Alternatives

> Case Study XIII: BF Skinner and Rosie the Riveter
>
> When the U.S. entered World War II, the country faced a serious problem. The U.S. armed forces required a large number of men. Many of the best men were working in heavy industry. Clearly before they could be taken away from their jobs, replacements would have to be found. The obvious choice was women. But in 1941 the idea that the "little woman" could move from baking cakes at home to producing tanks, artillery, war ships and bombers in large-scale factories seemed impossible.
>
> The behavioral psychologist BF Skinner had the answer. It was all a question of changing behavior. Where previously women involved in manual labor were thought to be part of the uneducated and poor lower class, relatively quickly women began to recognize they were the equal of their men fighting for the country. The women not only joined the workforce but developed a sense of accomplishment in their work.
>
> In today's machine-driven technology, we have forgotten that productivity is based on how workers feel about their work. If you treat a worker as a cog-in-a-machine, you cannot expect the machine to work efficiently.

Together with our workers, it is possible to develop an environment of worker empowerment where productivity rises to unequalled levels.

> Case Study XIV: The World's Shortest Lead Time
>
> In the late 1970s I was running a factory that produced quality silk dresses, skirts and blouses for designer labels. This was a special factory where all the sewers were multi-tasked craftsmen and everybody from the factory manager to the guy who swept the floor believed they personally were the world's greatest. Each person believed themselves responsible for the success of the operation.
>
> Our most important customer was Oscar de la Renta, a leading designer of the period. One Sunday morning in 1979, Oscar's partner Jerry Shaw telephoned with a very unusual request. Saks Fifth Avenue wanted to run a full-page ad the following Saturday featuring one of the styles we had yet to produce. How fast could we produce and ship? I told Jerry that I had to speak to my people and would call him back. Jerry already knew that I was a nutcase running some sort of commie operation where the workers made all the decisions. However, because of the quality, speed and reliability of the operation, he put up with me.
>
> I called everyone together – the factory manager, the department heads and the 15 sewing team leaders. Could we produce 550 dresses in 24 hours starting 9:30 Monday morning and goods finished and ready for pick-up on Tuesday at 9:00am?
>
> After a couple of hours, we made a deal. I would be responsible; they would do the best they could. Next question, how much? This took only 30 minutes (Chinese people can move to consensus very quickly, especially when money is involved): they wanted triple pay plus Tuesday, a holiday, also triple day. The head cutter disappeared. No fool. He was going to cut on the Sunday when all 10 tables were clear.

The Guide to Cost-to-Value Analysis

> Monday was a race against time. Every 30 minutes someone would run into the office telling me how well everything was moving, or how terrible was the latest disaster. Anyway, to make a long story short, we actually produced the 550 garments in 24 hours.
>
> When all is said and done it was not about the money. We must have lost $10,000, more if you include the disruption to the schedule.
>
> It was not about the customer. I could have refused. Even having done the impossible, Jerry was still certain that I was a pinko-liberal-commie nutcase.
>
> It certainly was not about me. Truth be told, my role was to sit on my office while everybody else did the work.
>
> It was about my people, who once again proved conclusively that from the manager down to the guy who sweeps the floor that they were indeed the greatest.
>
> This was 40 years ago. Those who are still around are long retired. Yet each one of them from time-to-time drags out the same story: You children with all your computers, machinery and all your fancy-schmancy education know nothing about work. Have I ever told you about the time when in one day, I. . . .

It is all about people.

Chapter 17
Technology III: The On-Demand Microfactory

We are grateful to Mr. Ram Sareen, Chief Coach & Founder of Tukatech, for the information in this chapter.

We tend to see new technology as a step forward, an improvement over the past. In many cases, technology is at best a solution to a problem we have created. For example, because we are working in countries with no qualified patternmakers, or we have lost our own skilled craftsmen patternmakers, we have developed computerized pattern making. But up to this time, computer-generated patterns are not as good as the old manually cut patterns although computer-generated patterns are better than no patterns at all.

More to the point, technological development has been piecemeal, breaking the process down in discrete steps, rather than looking at the process as a whole. The reality is that the whole is more than the sum of all steps. For example, whether specialized computerized robotic sewing machines are helpful depends on what you are producing. Robotic sewing machines are good if you are producing shirts or trousers, but fails if you are producing blouses or skirts because from the production point of view, all shirts and all trousers are the same while each blouse and skirt is different.

Finally, as with all innovation, the value of technology is not incremental improvement of the old but rather the ability to create something that never before has been possible. There are a few tech companies today looking at such comprehensive development. One of the most interesting efforts comes from Tukatech and its on-demand microfactory.

This is a wholistic solution. Where others are moving to replace people with machines, Tukatech's goal is to provide people with better tools. At the same time, rather than break down the process into discrete steps, the on-demand microfactory is the entire supply chain in a single room.

This is also an ongoing process and there are of course problems. Tukatech is working to solve those problems to bring the system closer to reality. The company recognizes that being the best is not enough.

The on-demand microfactory has four interrelated goals, all of which seek to reduce costs on both the customer and factory/supplier sides. They are:

    a.   Shift product development from the customer to the supplier;

    b.   Provide factory fast turn and quick response capability;

The Guide to Cost-to-Value Analysis

    c. Reduce lead times to the point when the factory can produce both first orders and re-orders immediately after receipt of customer's order;

    d. By ensuring a, b and c, markdown can then be reduced to a point approaching zero.

The operation includes a number of variations and modules, depending on the customer's needs, but the process always begins with the same first step: CUSTOMER'S DESIGNER PROVIDES INITIAL DESIGN. After that, the factory takes over. Here's the flow chart of the steps involved:

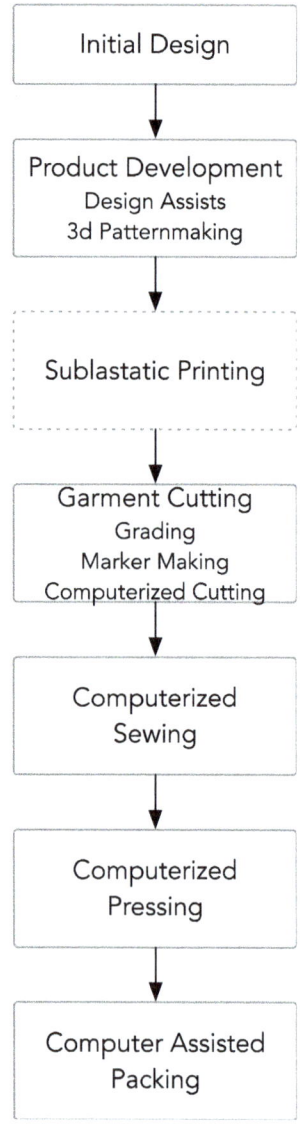

Chapter 17 Technology III: The On-Demand Microfactory

PRODUCT DEVELOPMENT includes converting the designer's sketch into a computer-generated photograph in the right fabric worn by a model, followed by a 3D pattern. From there, if required, the on-demand microfactory can produce actual samples.

If required, the system is equipped with an on-demand digital printing module that permits the widest range of designs and colorways to be added to the fabric in minutes. This is particularly useful for plaids, engineered patterns and other prints that require vertical and horizontal matching.

GARMENT CUTTING includes computer-generated grading, computer-generated marker making and computer-generated cutting. One important factor is the system's ability to grade a large number of sizes. For example, instead of only waist sizes 32-34-36 in pants, the factory can provide 30-31-32-33-34-35-36 at no extra cost to their retailer customer. The same occurs with inseam measurement. As a result, the retailer can offer a much wider range of sizes and has a much higher probability of being able to give the consumer their exact size without any need for alterations.

This is where technology can provide what is known as disruptive innovation. When we combine virtually infinite sizing with speed to market, for the first time production can truly follow daily retail sales. The consumer receives the closest thing to a bespoke garment on a timely basis while the retailer carries zero inventory.

Once the fabric is ready, the on-demand microfactory allows for at least two important variations in COMPUTERIZED SEWING depending on the product. For simple styles such as shirts, pants and skirts, very fast production coupled with worker training can take place in a very short period of time.

For more complex designs and production for products such as dresses, coats and jackets, sewing teams with highly skilled, multi-tasked sewers are used instead of computerized machinery. The sewing teams are more flexible than computerized machinery allowing for increased production without major capital outlays. The problem here is that while the computerized-machine operator can be trained in a matter of days, training of multi-tasked sewers may require 12-18 months.

The problem of multi-tasked worker training time could be solved by using existing tailors who are becoming unemployed as customers shift from bespoke to branded label clothing.

The Guide to Cost-to-Value Analysis

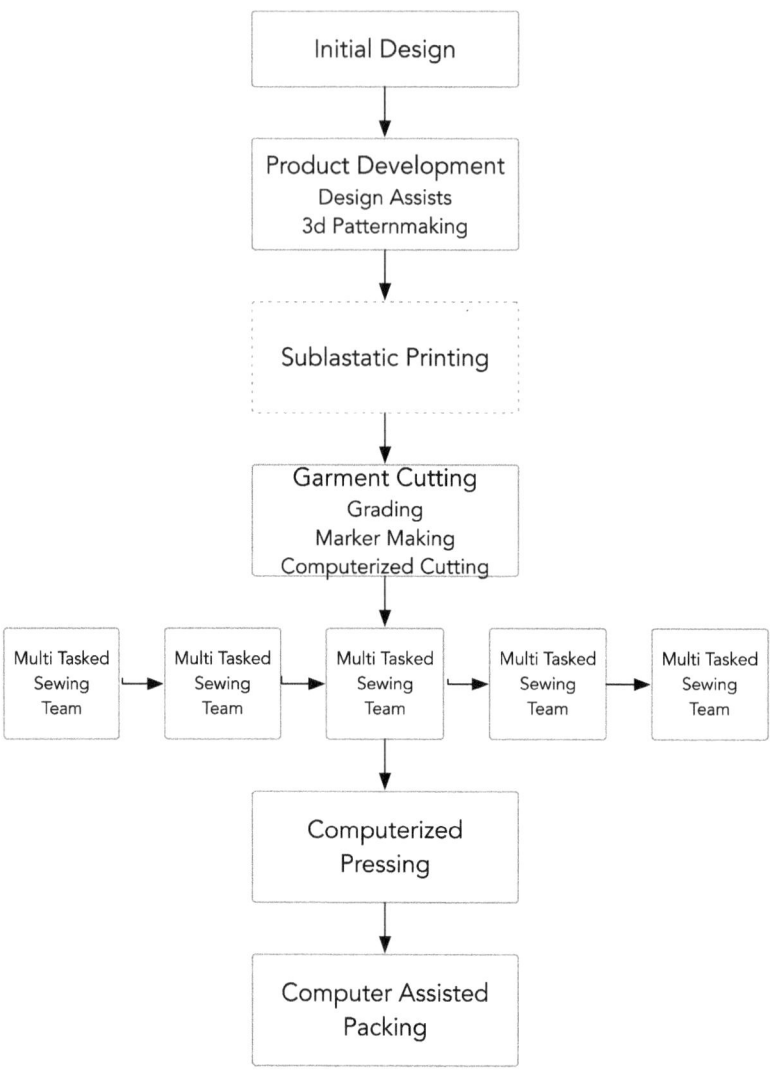

The on-demand microfactory offers total multi-dimensional flexibility:

- The system operates equally effectively in factories producing as few as 250 garments per day and as many as 5000+ per day.

- Because of the great cost savings (as we will see below), the factory can be located anywhere in the world and shipping everywhere in the world. The cost savings are so great that airfreight costs are easily absorbed.

For more information on Tukatech, here is the link to their website:
https://www.tukatech.com/downloads/Video/End-to-End_Solutions.mp4

Chapter 17 Technology III: The On-Demand Microfactory

In the real world, innovation, no matter how exciting and alluring, will not be accepted until the benefits can be quantified. So let's look at the following COST-TO-VALUE cost sheet.

	Cost-to-Value Cost Sheet: On-Demand Microfactory				
		I No Product Development No Markdown Reduction		II With Product Development + Markdown Reduction	
Item		Factors	Cost	Cost	Factors
1	Material		$6.00	$6.00	
2	Trim		$1.00	$1.00	
3	CM Labor		$0.64	$0.64	
4	CM Overhead		$1.86	$1.86	
5	Cost of Service: Product Development		$0.00	$0.25	
6	Cost of Service: Markdown Reduction		$0.00	$1.00	
7	CM Total Cost		$2.50	$3.75	
8	Total Factory Cost		$9.50	$10.75	
9	Added Value Product Development		$0.00	$0.50	
10	Added Value Markdown Reduction		$0.00	$2.00	
11	Net Factory Profit	5.0%	$0.50	$3.00	30.0%
12	Total FOB Cost		$10.00	$13.75	
13	Agent Commission	5.0%	$0.50	$0.69	5.0%
14	Freight		$0.25	$0.25	
15	Duty	16.2%	$1.62	$2.23	16.2%
16	Clearance		$0.10	$0.10	
17	Transport		$0.15	$0.15	
18	Total DDP		$12.62	$16.67	
19	Product Development Loading	20.0%	$2.52	$0.83	5.0%
20	Distribution Center Loading	5.0%	$0.63	$0.83	5.0%
21	In-Store		$15.78	$18.33	
22	Markup	75.0%	$47.33	$44.77	70.1%
23	Retail		$63.10	$63.10	
24	Markdown	33.0%	$20.82	$3.16	5.0%
25	Net Retail		$42.28	$59.95	
26	Net Retailer Profit		$26.50	$41.61	$15.11

The Guide to Cost-to-Value Analysis

Item 5: Cost of Product Development service
    I: $0.00 No added cost
    II: $0.25 While the factory can quantify the total cost of product development, it is impossible to determine the cost per unit until the factory knows the size of the order. The $0.25 above assumes a total cost of $500 for an order of 2000 pieces.

Item 6: Cost of Markdown Reduction service
    I: $0.00 No added cost
    II $1.00 This is calculated directly on a per unit basis.

Item 9: Added Value Product Development service
    I: $0.00 No added value
    II: $0.50 This is an arbitrary but not unreasonable amount.

Item10: Added Value Markdown Reduction service
    I: $0.00 No added value
    II: $2.00 This is an arbitrary but as we will see below a not unreasonable amount.

Item 11: Net Factory Profit:
    I: $0.50 Normal net profit of 5% of FOB
    II: $3.00 This is initial $0.50 profit + $0.50 added profit for product development service + $2.00 added profit for markdown reduction service.

Item 19: Product Development Loading
    I: $2.52 Few if any retailers or brands calculate the actual per unit cost of product development. The best they can do is to calculate aggregate cost of product development as a percentage of total DDP cost and take that result as a loading of usually 20% of DDP.
    II: $0.83 The customer's designer does carry out some portion of work (see above INITIAL DESIGN). The 5% is purely an estimate, probably in excess of actual costs.

Item 21: In-store cost. This is the total of the garment costs up to the point when it arrives at the store.
    I: $15.78 (sum of items 18-20)
    II: $18.33 (sum of items 18-20)

From this point forward, calculations are based on the retailer's pricing decisions. While the in-store cost (Item 18) of I is $4.05 ($16.67 - $12.62) less than II, management is aware that once markdown costs have been factored in, factory services will provide a much more substantial cost saving. The question remains is what is to be done with this savings. The range of possibilities extends from RETAILER RETAINS 100% OF SAVINGS AS ADDED PROFIT to RETAILER RETAINS 0% OF SAVINGS GIVING 100% OF THE BENEFIT TO THE CONSUMER IN THE FORM OF REDUCED RETAIL PRICE.

For the purpose of this exercise we will assume that the retailer retains 100% of the savings. So the explanation of the rest of the cost-to-value cost sheet runs as follows:

Chapter 17 Technology III: The On-Demand Microfactory

Item 22: Markup
  I: $47.33. The customer works on 75% gross markup.
  II: $47.33. The customer adds the same amount in order to retain 100% of the cost savings.

Item 23: Retail price (sum of items 21 + 22)
  I: $63.10
  II: $63.10

Item 24: Markdown
  I: $20.82 = 33% of retail. Given the current retail environment this is a not unreasonable amount.
  II: $3.16 = 5% of retail. Although the initial concept is to move to 0% markdowns, we should allow for some problems.

Item 25: Net retail price (item 23 less item 24)
  I: $42.28
  II: $59.95

Item 26: Net retailer profit (item 25 less item 21)
  I: $26.50
  II: $41.61

$15.11: Net retailer savings from factory services ($41.61 less $26.50)

What the cost-to-value cost sheet shows us is this is a true win/win situation for both the factory and the customer.

- The factory's profit increases from 5% to 30% of FOB.

- The customer saves $15 on a garment with an FOB price of $10. It would be as if the factory were paying his customer $5 for the privilege of making his garments.

This then takes us back to the original thesis of the cost-to-value concept. The cost of any product is really irrelevant to the customer. The customer cares only about value.

Chapter 18
Cost-to-Value Analysis or the Ultimate Cost Sheet

This book is about costs and prices, how they are related and mostly about a methodology to compare one with the other to determine profit for both the customer and his supplier.

Remember, cost is what the supplier pays. Price is what the customer pays.

Cost and price are unrelated in the sense that while cost is based on what the supplier pays for materials and work, price is based on the value that the customer places on the finished product and, as we have seen, value is very subjective. But cost and price are related in the sense that the price the supplier pays for a particular item immediately becomes an important cost determining the price he will charge his customer.

The role of the cost sheet is to compare cost with price (or value) to determine the best way forward in the selection of best supplier, best investment, or best business strategy. We have seen that the traditional basic cost sheet model is both incomplete and fundamentally flawed and therefore does not provide the information both the supplier and his customer need. It is equally clear that the cost sheet template that would meet the needs of the industry is both necessary and very complex.

At this point, we can all understand an accurate cost sheet – one based on the cost and value of any new service or investment by either the customer or his factory supplier – requires accurate input from both sides. Incomplete data or fake data destroys the entire costing model.

The greatest problem is that the decision-making process, particularly on the customer side, is often irrational. An appreciable percentage of customers still holds fast to the FOB-price-over-all competitive model. There is no evidence that low FOB price results in higher retailer or brand profit but importers continue fighting for lower FOB prices because that is what importers have always done. This is what psychologists term ARRESTED DEVELOPMENT. The IF-BUT crowd is even less rational. They accept that value-added services are important, while simultaneously rejecting the full-service factories capable of delivering those services because those factories have higher FOB prices.

Today customers select factories based on a scoreboard. They list 10 factors on which they rate factory suppliers including location, membership in free-trade-agreements (FTA), lead times, quality, reliability and financial standing. These are all real and important factors but there is actually no way that these factors together will arrive at a list of the best factories.

The Guide to Cost-to-Value Analysis

The problem is that the customer's list is an attempt to pre-determine WHY some suppliers are better than others yet the fundamental problem is that we do not know why. The answer to why does not belong in any rational decision-making process. If you want to know why, go to your local church, synagogue, mosque or temple and ask your minister, rabbi, imam, lama or pujari. The WHY is their business. For the rest of us, knowing WHAT is the best we can do.

Imagine we had a way, using existing data, to determine which is the best factory or which is the best customer. First, we have to define BEST CUSTOMER or BEST SUPPLIER. Let's assume that the best customer/supplier is the one where we make the most money. We no longer care about CMT, FOB or DDP. We care only about NET.

For the factory, the solution is found in Chapter 1. If the job costing sheets have been completed and the factory has moved to a unit cost accounting system, it is possible to calculate the net profit of every order. Averaging them out by customer gives net profit for each customer. The computer can also give net profit for each product and each month.

For the customer, there is an equally practical solution:

1. Determine total cost up to In-Store Delivery

		End-to-End Costing: FOB to In-Store Delivery for 10000 units			
1	Total FOB Cost			$10.00	$100,000
2	Agent Commission	5.0%		$0.50	$5,000
3	Freight			$0.25	$2,500
4	Duty	16.2%		$1.62	$16,200
5	Clearance			$0.10	$1,000
6	Transport			$0.15	$1,500
7	Total DDP			$12.62	$126,200
8	Product Development Loading	20.0%		$2.52	$25,240
9	Distribution Center Loading	5.0%		$0.63	$6,310
10	In-Store Delivery			$15.78	$157,750

2. Determine total net receipts after all sales and discounts

	Net Retail 10,000 Units			
Net Retail Price			$56.79	$422,800
Net Retail Profit	64.2%		$36.47	$364,700

Chapter 18 Cost-to-Value Analysis or the Ultimate Cost Sheet

Bear in mind that all the necessary data exists. We need only aggregate the results to determine the average profit from each factory over a period of time.

3. Further analysis allows us to determine just how this profit was achieved by compiling a full value cost sheet.

The FOB costs are transferred from the first markdown costing sheet from Chapter 11 where the factory earns $3.00 more per unit providing services such as trial orders and quick response which allow the customer to reduce markdowns by, in this case, 33%. Here again is a table showing how much cost savings the customer achieves through reduced markdowns.

		Full Value Cost Sheet: Added Factory Service			
		No Added Service		With Added Service	
		Factors	Costs	Costs	Factors
1	Total FOB Cost		$10.00	$13.00	
2	Agent Commission	5.0%	$0.50	$0.65	5.0%
3	Freight		$0.25	$0.25	
4	Duty	16.2%	$1.62	$2.11	16.2%
5	Clearance		$0.10	$0.10	
6	Transport		$0.15	$0.15	
7	Total DDP		$12.62	$16.26	
8	Product Development Loading	20.0%	$2.52	$3.25	20.0%
9	Distribution Center Loading	5.0%	$0.63	$0.81	5.0%
10	In-Store		$15.78	$20.32	
11	Markup	75.0%	$47.33	$42.78	67.8%
12	Retail		$63.10	$63.10	
13	**Markdown**	33.0%	$20.82	$6.31	10.0%
14	Net Retail		$42.28	$56.79	
15	**Net Customer Profit**		$26.50	$36.47	$9.97

Cost-to-Value Sourcing

The purpose of cost-to-value sourcing is not to replace the merchandiser but rather to provide the tools to allow the merchandiser to make better decisions. Currently, using the old sourcing methods, a customer placing each month 5000 orders in 1000 factories located in 12 countries must rely on guesswork.

In order to fully benefit from cost-to-value sourcing, each customer should

The Guide to Cost-to-Value Analysis

create a customized database meeting their individual needs by criteria such as:

   a. Breakdown by supplying country;
   b. Breakdown by quantity: There is a substantial difference between a factory delivering 50,000-500,000 pieces and a factory delivering 500-2000 pieces of the same style;
   c. Further breakdown by product: There is a substantial difference between an unlined denim jacket factory and one capable of making a lined worsted blazer.

Cost-to-value sourcing along with its full value cost sheet provides detailed cost information in real time and becomes the first step in a more accurate sourcing process. We must understand that providing added profit, while an important consideration, may not always be the measure of the best results. An example where added profits is not the most important yardstick is in products where quality trumps everything. Another example is in regards to strategic suppliers who are guaranteed steady business in pre-specified quantities throughout the year. In these cases, the merchandiser will weigh the special requirements along with the greatest profit criteria.

Cost-to-value sourcing provides a number of special tools that were previously unavailable, allowing for greater analysis of changes in sourcing patterns and results. Let's say a factory which provided 65% net profit last year is down to 55%. The customer and sourcing team should examine the reason for that decline. Another example could be studying a cost-reduction service provided by one factory and whether it might be something the customer should replicate in other factories that it is working with.

Gone are the days where sourcing success was based primarily on achieving the lowest FOB cost. Intelligent apparel sourcing today must be based on full value costing as well as cost-to-value analysis.

Chapter 19
Branding the Supplier Side

Partnership is the single most important factor defining the collaborative model. What is true for the individual company as in the case of the universal factory supplier (see Chapter 22) or the new SME sector (see Chapter 21) is equally true of entire national industries. But here there is an important consideration. When we speak of partnership with a national garment-exporting industry, just who are we partnering with?

Throughout this book we have looked at everything as a two-party relationship between the customer (importer, retailer, and brand) and the supplier (factory).

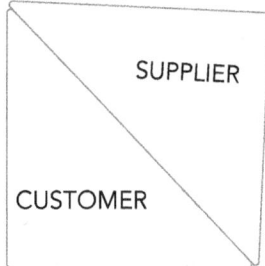

Today, however, our industry is now in a tripartite relationship which includes not only the customer and supplier but also the consumer.

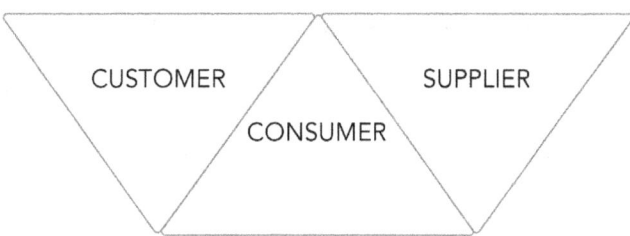

More importantly, we are operating in a buyers' market, where the consumer is dominant. We think we understand the nature of the buyers' market. After all most of us were around in 2009 when General Motors went bankrupt. Some of us can even recall the statement by Charles Wilson, the head of GM and later US Secretary of Defense, who said: "What is good for General Motors is good for America". In 52 years GM went from the world's greatest corporation down to nothing simply because what GM was selling, consumers were not buying. Big, big shock.

With this in mind, it might make more sense that rather than forming a partnership with the customer, suppliers would do well to form their partnership with the consumer. As with any marketing strategy, success depends on two things: *Find*

The Guide to Cost-to-Value Analysis

out what your customer wants. Give it to them.

To a large degree, today's consumers want what they have always wanted: good design, good make, good material at the right price. That alone does not help us. Today's consumer wants more: greater CSR and compliance, sustainability, transparency. Once again, that's no secret. Every retailer and every brand has been rushing to re-brand themselves as responsible people, preaching the new CSR gospel, joining the latest organization dedicated to CSR, extolling in the loudest voice: TRUST US. WE ARE ONE OF THE GOOD GUYS!

Indeed, some retailers and brands really are the good guys, having followed ethical behavior before CSR became the flavor of the month. Others, recognizing the shift in the consumer wind, have joined the battle for change. They too deserve credit. Recently some retailers and brands have even started publishing the names and locations of their factory suppliers inviting consumers to visit their factories. They have not had many takers. And then there are the rest: many if not most customers still look at ethics as a gimmick, just one more label to stick on their garments.

Whatever the strategies to convince consumers that the garments are indeed made by compliant suppliers, the retailers and brands are failing to convince consumers. The primary reason is that the new generation of consumers led by the millennials – those troublemaking nihilists – are not buying either the messages or the products. These young people have been brought up in an atmosphere of lies, more lies and advertising and they reject any attempt by retailers or brands to push their products.

These new consumers use social media to decide where to buy what. If they want body care products, rather than reading the advertising copy published by the big cosmetic labels, they go to social media where every product type is analyzed in depth. Which are those with toxic chemicals to be avoided? What are the active ingredients and how much of these ingredients are in each product? Why pay $250 for some big label product when some company in Canada or South Korea is selling something better for $26.

Social media INFLUENCERS are no longer middle-aged actors dressed up in professional coats playing doctor or dentist. They are young people who have taken it on themselves to tell-it-like-it-is. Some social media influencers have millions of followers. The rules governing influencers are very strict. Taking money from companies to tout their products is a no-no. One mistake and the company or brand goes on a consumer black list.

Retailers and brands face a second problem. When they claim to be socially responsible, they are not referring to themselves but rather to their factory suppliers. It is not that consumers believe that retailers and brands have to argue that they do not employ ten-year-old children in sweatshop conditions in their New York or London headquarters. When bragging about their high-

Chapter 19 Branding the Supplier Side

level social responsibility they are referring to workers in their factories located in Bangladesh, India and Cambodia. To the millennials these claims are risible. Since the retailers and brands are not trusted to begin with, any claim they make that some factory in Dhaka is compliant or sustainable won't be believed just because the company says so. If anything, such a claim would put the factory supplier on a list of suspect suppliers.

Rebranding the retailer or brand is virtually impossible unless your name is Marks & Spencer or Levi Strauss, companies with well-known reputations for ethical behavior dating back generations. Of course, these companies need not rebrand themselves because they already carry the ethical brand. For the others, rebranding is very difficult, even with the greatest effort. They face insurmountable obstacles.

First of all, they start with negative reputations. As a group, retailers and brands have a history of untrustworthy behavior. Before rebranding themselves as ethical companies, they have to change consumers' perceptions of their past. Telling people, "*This is who we were, but we have changed*" is a long and arduous task, with little chance of success.

Secondly, they have no way to ensure their suppliers are and will remain ethical. Major importers may be working with 500-1000+ factories located in a dozen or more countries. The moment one factory is caught with children or has a fire, the bad reputation that the importer began with is reinforced and their efforts, even if real, are perceived as yet one more attempt to fool the consumer.

There exists a viable practical solution to this dilemma. Although the retailer or brand customer cannot be reliably branded, the supplier factory can. It is simply a question of making information regarding factory suppliers available to the consumer. Up to now the factory has remained anonymous. Every consumer knows the brand Tommy Hilfiger, but who has heard of any of their factory suppliers?

Branding the Factory: The Strategy

The process begins with three or four factories located in the same area. They need not be perfect, but they should be decent operations. The factory begins with a clean slate upon which it can then build its reputation.

These are the steps the factory should follow:

> 1. Make contact with two or three legitimate and well-recognized social networking influencers. Invite them to travel to your home country to visit the factory. Pay for their travel expenses but assure them there is no *quid pro quo* expected. Don't make them sit through any stock Power Point presentations. Management should be available to answer any questions that the influencers have. They should be allowed to go anywhere they

want and talk to anyone in the factory. The factory will provide a university graduate to act as translator, if necessary.

2. Ask only that the social networking influencers, on return to their home country, write an honest description of what they saw, both the good and the bad.

3. Six months later bring the social networking influencers back to see for themselves the effects of their trips and subsequent comments. This could result in ongoing dialogue and positive developments such as:

- Influencer's Criticism: Factories employ predominantly women age 18-25, more than likely recently married with small children, but the women have nobody to look after their children.
- Factory's Response: We approached foreign governments and international institutions for help. They recommended a team of professionals to design our day care center and train our staff. The building is almost complete. On your follow-up visit, we will introduce you to the professionals retained to carry out the work. Talk to them and discuss the progress, the problems and solutions. We invite you to stay in touch with them to ensure that all is going as expected.

- Influencer's Criticism: No labor unions.
- Factory's Response: This is a difficult problem, one which is somewhat outside our control. We cannot work independently. We need the support of our national industry organization and the government. Initiating a labor union movement has been difficult everywhere but we are moving ahead. We have brought in representatives from the International Labor Organization (ILO), a United Nations agency, and Solidarity, the international arm of the U.S.-based AFL/CIO. Together we have formulated a plan to bring about a local labor union movement. This will not be an easy or short-term strategy, but we are confident that it will be successful. We invite you to meet again with our partners in the next room on your next visit. Continue to discuss the issues with them and please follow up to ensure that we are moving forward.

- Influencer's Criticism: Excessive overtime.
- Factory's Response: Unfortunately we cannot solve this problem. Ours is a seasonal industry. We cannot build a factory based only on working during the high season just as we cannot solve the problem of not having enough orders during the slow periods. But we are moving ahead to at least ameliorate the problem of excessive overtime. We now limit overtime to 25% which means our 48-hour week allows for 12 hours maximum overtime weekly. Furthermore we guarantee our workers overtime pay and one day off each week. We accept that we should do better. We can say only that as of yet, we cannot do better.

Chapter 19   Branding the Supplier Side

4. The factory has now taken concrete steps to brand their company:

- The legitimate social networking influencers have worked to change the industry from the consumer side and to a large extent have succeeded. Through the efforts of the factories, the role of the influencers has moved from local to global. The day care center, the labor union movement and even the reduction in overtime (although still unacceptable) is the direct result of their efforts. They are creating "good" factories.
- By being 100% open and honest, the factories have created trust between the factory supplier and the consumer. In a buyers' market where the consumers operate in a culture of informed cynicism, the very existence of trustworthy factories is a giant step forward.
- Retailers and brands now have a few factories recognized as ethical by independent evaluators. These factories will attract customers and in doing so, bring other factories into the system. What began as a small group will soon grow. In as little as five years, an entire national industry could be branded.

All this depends on maintaining the strictest standards of ethical behavior. What is suggested in this chapter won't take factories operating decades in the past and catapult them into the future in six short months. But factories currently exist in every country that are more than able to meet the high standards required for the self-branding strategy. By following the steps outlined above, they can certainly increase their customer base and profits by going directly to the consumer.

Chapter 20
Decline of Brick and Mortar and the Rise of E-Commerce

E-commerce is taking over garment retail. E-commerce currently comes in three flavors:

    a. E-commerce giants
    b. E-commerce as an extension of brick and mortar (B&M) retail
    c. Small e-commerce start-ups

For the first two categories, e-commerce is simply computerized B&M. Both the traditional B&M sector and the e-commerce giants follow the same classic something-for-everybody business model based on the need for ever-increasing market share. The B&M players were forced into the model because their sales are limited by the distance the potential consumer will travel to visit one of their stores. To maximize its customer base the store must sell fashion that appeals to the greatest number of potential customers and at prices that will further attract those customers. But today the something-for-everybody model defined as fashion-for-everybody strategy has put the major B&M retailers in a hole. Problems such as ever-increasing markdowns and boring design can be traced directly back to this need for ever greater market share. The e-commerce giants chose the same strategy with similar results.

But the advent of the small e-commerce start-ups has changed everything:

Fable: The Origin of E-Commerce Start-ups

E-commerce began with one person: Tom with the big head.

Tom wore a size 72 hat, or would have, if there had been a size 72 hat. The problem is that only one man in a million has Tom's size head. If a store is located in a large urban area with a potential consumer base of 10,000,000, of which half or 5,000,000 are men, a store selling size 72 hats would have five potential customers. We can understand why Tom went hatless.

Until the day Tom saw the internet and went into business himself. With the internet, Tom's customer base was not a circle with a 50-mile radius. It was a circle with a radius of 12,500 miles. His customer base was not 10,000,000, it was now 7,000,000,000. And instead of only five potential customers, Tom had 3,500 potential customers, every one of which would be willing to pay a premium for a hat that actually fit their big (or super small) head.

Tom set up a website, went to a hat factory where he placed orders for size 72 hats in four styles, 500 pieces each. A month later, the hats arrived at Tom's house. He put his stock in his garage, his guest room, in fact everywhere.

The Guide to Cost-to-Value Analysis

> He posted the stuff on his website and sat back and waited. The first day he sold three hats. By the end of the first month he had sold 43 hats. This was a little depressing until one of the social media superstars posted two sentences on Instagram:
>
> TOM WITH BIG HEAD SELLS SIZE 72 MEN'S HATS! GO TO TOMWITHBIGHEAD.COM!!
> The good news was that Tom's business dramatically increased. The bad news was that Tom's stock sold out in 34 minutes.
>
> Tom's business plan was different. Rather than measuring success in terms of rising market share, Tom was happy with a market share of 0.000001%. In Tom's new market, success is based entirely on the product that is new, exciting and, above all, different. Tom's business model could be summed up in one very strange sentence: THE SMALLER YOUR CUSTOMER BASE, THE MORE SUCCESSFUL YOUR OPERATION.
>
> This is the fundamental problem facing the something-for-everybody crowd. The big stores all have e-commerce websites, but what they are selling is by definition cookie-cutter boring. Tom's customers shun them. In fact, their only customers are the people who already shop those brick and mortar stores.
>
> Think of garment retail as a three-tiered market. At the top we have the designer labels. At the bottom we have the mass-market Walmarts and Targets. Both have secure customer bases. The big brick and mortar stores are in the middle. They not only have to compete against the top and the bottom tiers, but also against Tom-with-the-big-head and his thousands of friends who have set up similar small e-commerce businesses.
>
> Where once retail was blah, suddenly the design cutting-edge now extends out to infinity. Today anybody with an idea could actually go into business. Of course, 90% go broke in the first year, but the new generation something-for-somebody has definitely caught on and many of the new small e-commerce businesses are quite successful.

As with most fables, the story of Tom-with-the-big-head is either not true or totally true.

Chapter 21
Developing the New SME E-Commerce Supplier Sector

The global garment-export industry is for the most part family-run and is now in its second generation. Even those running the largest billion-dollar transnational factory groups can remember how their fathers began their companies. In the early days ours was an industry built for Asia-based small and medium-size enterprises (SMEs) who enjoyed low capital investment requirements and relied on cheap semi-skilled labor. Everyone has his own story:

> We began in Sri Lanka with a dry goods store. My grandfather decided to build a small factory to produce garments for his store.

> I was a teacher in Mauritius. My wife and I together with our accountant opened a 30-machine factory. We almost went broke with our first order.

You want to hear stories? Go to Hong Kong, the very center of the global garment-export industry. The stories there come in three dialects: Shanghainese, Cantonese and Chiu Chow. Everyone arrived in Hong Kong as a refugee. Some came by air, others by train and not a few directly by water – they swam in. Some, mainly Shanghainese, came with capital. Others with nothing except knowledge, experience and the ability to work hard. Separately, or together, they built the world's largest and most successful export-garment industry.

The advent of quota limitations on exports from the major garment-exporting countries opened the door for SME factories located in quota-free countries. By the time quotas were phased out in 2005, just about every country in the world had developed garment-exporting industries that included large numbers of SME factories.

Eventually the tide shifted. With too many factories chasing too few customers, many factories, particularly SMEs, were driven out of business. At the same time, retail consolidation in garment-importing countries drove their customers, the SME retailers, out of business. The cost of new technology coupled with customer demand for special services requiring additional highly skilled technicians made SMEs even less competitive. The end of quota in 2005 seemingly brought a close to the era of SME factory start-ups worldwide.

But just as the SME factory sector was coming to an end, a new SME customer sector was coming into existence. This new sector would not only keep the small factories alive but could potentially make those factories the most successful sector in the global garment-exporting industry. The new SME e-commerce start-ups need SME factory suppliers since their volumes are too small to work with the large factory groups. The collaborative model partnership ensures that

The Guide to Cost-to-Value Analysis

the relationship of these customers and suppliers can thrive.

There is therefore an urgent need to develop SME factories to meet the special needs of the new emerging SME e-commerce sector, the fastest developing sector in the global garment industry. But right now there are many obstacles to achieving this potential. Among the most serious is the inability of e-commerce companies to work effectively with factory suppliers, just as SME factories are unable to meet the needs of the potential SME e-commerce buyers.

ANY NATIONAL INDUSTRY CAPABLE OF OVERCOMING THESE OBSTACLES WILL BECOME THE WORLD LEADER IN THIS IMPORTANT NEW SECTOR.

The way forward is to create a national SME Center that will provide the necessary services, assistance and training to allow both the SME factories and their potential SME e-commerce customers to flourish. The following shows steps in the supply chain where obstacles exist and how the national SME Center can provide the means to remove those obstacles.

1. Fabric Sourcing

    a. Obstacle: The quantity of fabric required is too small to order directly from most mills. This leaves the SME e-commerce companies with only two alternatives: limit themselves to commodity fabric only or use the limited variety of fashion fabric available for which they must pay a hefty premium.

    b. Solution: There does exist an almost inexhaustible quantity and variety of fashion fabric available at well below market price. Every garment factory and every fabric mill has quantities of "dead" fabric, usually left over from orders previously shipped. Therefore, a market does exist, but there is no marketplace. The national SME Center would create a virtual online marketplace where fabric types categorized by product type – shirting, trouser weights, suitings – would be further cross divided by fiber – cotton, synthetic, wool. Customers could order swatches for a nominal fee, sample fabric of 5-10mts at a premium, and finally stock fabric at the best prices. The center's fabric marketplace would charge a small commission for each purchase.

Chapter 21 Developing the New SME E-Commerce Supplier Sector

Virtual Fabric Marketplace

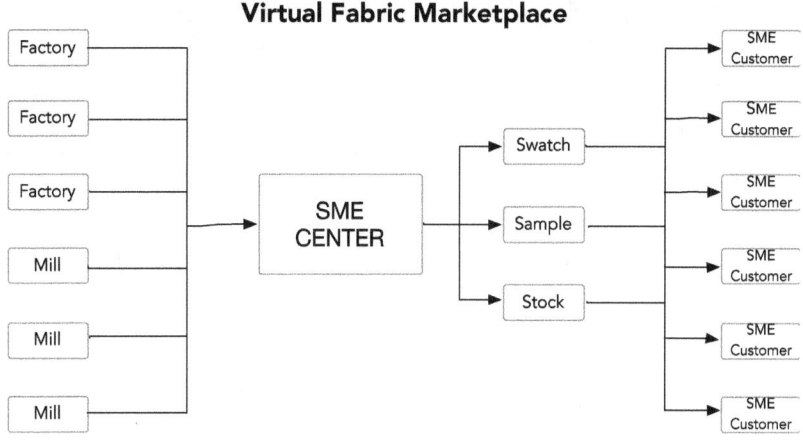

2. Pattern making, grading and marker making

a. Obstacle: Based on 14 styles per day (with average two cuttings for each style), no SME factory has the in-house capacity to carry out pattern making, grading and marker making. There are excellent high-speed computer systems that can produce the work efficiently and in large quantities, but the costs are beyond the means of any SME factory.

b. Solution: The SME Center creates a sector-wide high-tech pattern-making, grading and marker-making facility which can carry out the work at a reasonable cost and send the results to each factory via internet.

Pattern-Making, Grading and Marker-Making Facility

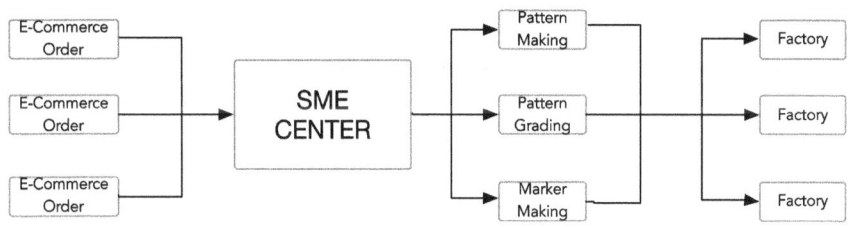

3. Fast-turn production for small quantities

a. Obstacle: Most SME factories are currently geared to act as subcontractors with workers divided into lines producing relatively large quantities of a few styles. Because of the factory structure and system, factories are trapped at the very bottom. This is probably the greatest cause of sweatshop operations paying slave labor rates.

b. Solution: The national SME Center would provide engineers to move the factory from lines using single-tasked semi-skilled workers into teams employing multi-tasked sewers. Through the center's work, the sweatshop factories can become totally compliant operations with the highest standards of sustainability and total transparency.

The Guide to Cost-to-Value Analysis

Engineering and Training Facility

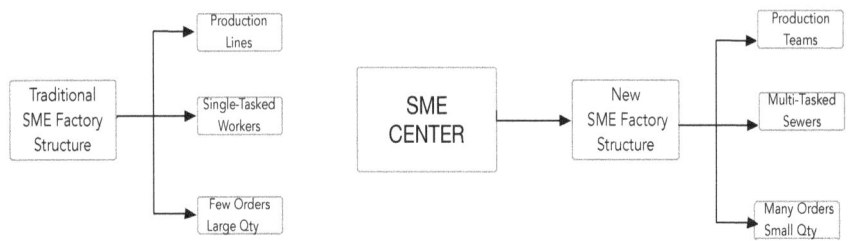

4. Pick & Pack consolidation and final shipment to the consumer

a. Obstacle: The logistics are extremely complex and do not work well in an SME operation.

  i. Pick & pack for 200-400 individual consumer orders daily is a very expensive proposition for an SME factory.
  ii. Goods could be shipped from the factory directly to the consumer but the cost would be prohibitive. To be cost-effective, shipments to individual consumers should first be consolidated and then shipped to four or five separate locations where the final pick & pack process takes place with the orders sent on to each individual consumer.
  iii. An SME factory does not have the facilities necessary to carry out the process.

b. Solution: The national SME Center creates a single automated facility to service the entire sector.

Traditional Pick & Pack

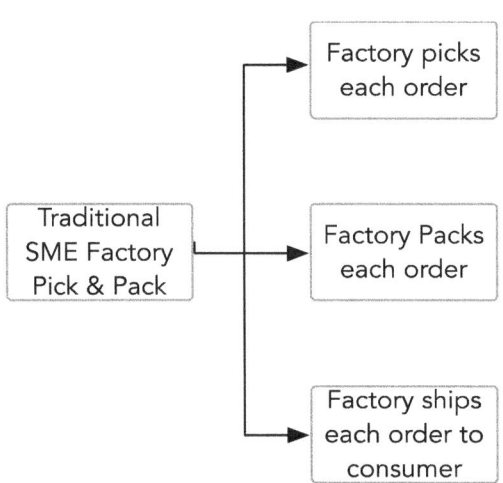

112

Chapter 21 Developing the New SME E-Commerce Supplier Sector

New Model Pick & Pack

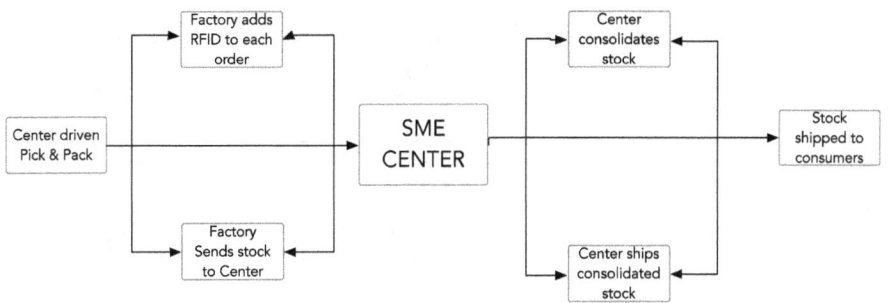

The move from the individual base where factories and their e-commerce customers act as single entities to the sector base where everyone acts together through the SME Center provides benefits to all.

1. The SME factory benefits by concentrating on those operations best suited to the individual factory, while passing on all other operations to the SME Center, thus increasing productivity. At the same time, the SME factory learns the techniques necessary to escape from the zero-service factory trap. The result is a larger customer base and substantially greater per unit profit.

2. The SME e-commerce company benefits by limiting its work to original design and marketing while at the same time reducing costs by passing on other operations to those more capable, more efficient and, most importantly, more able to provide economies of scale. The result is less work coupled with greater profit.

3. The national industry benefits. Where once the SME factory sector was forced to operate with poor compliance, lack of sustainability and zero transparency, the SME Center is able to ensure that all participating SME factories meet the highest ethical standards. Most importantly, because of the growing number of SME e-commerce companies, this project is highly scalable.

4. The SME Center will be a profit-making operation thus ensuring that outside funding will only be required for the initial investment.

The left side of the following comparison cost sheet shows typical costs for a small e-commerce company producing in their home country and paying premium prices for fabric that they source on their own from limited local suppliers. On the right side, the e-commerce company shifts production to an offshore SME factory which works with a national SME Center that offers an online fabric marketplace of leftover fabric sold at discounted prices and centralized pick & pack services.

The Guide to Cost-to-Value Analysis

Costs for E-commerce Company at Home Country Factory vs Offshore SME Factory				
		By E-commerce company at home	By offshore SME factory	
Fabric		$6.00	$3.00	
Trim		$1.00	$1.00	
CM Labor		$7.00	$0.64	
CM Overhead	70%	$4.90	$1.86	290%
Cost of Pick & Pack Service		$0.00	$0.10	
Total Cost		$18.90	$6.60	
Service Charge from SME Center			$1.32	20%
Factory Net Profit		$1.89	$3.00	
Total FOB		$20.79	$10.92	
Freight In		$1.00	$0.00	
Freight Out		$2.00	$2.00	
Pick & Pack		$1.00	$1.00	
Cost Shipped to Consumer		$24.90	$13.92	$10.98

The benefit to both sides is substantial: the customer's cost drops from $24.90 to $13.92 per unit while the factory's net profit increases from $1.89 (assume 10% of FOB) to $3.00. Of course, developing the SME sector so that it can work efficiently with the new e-commerce sector customers will require some investment and substantial training in the factory suppliers' countries.

Chapter 22
The Universal Factory Supplier

It is possible for a factory located anywhere in the world to become a strategic supplier to a major retailer also located anywhere in the world provided that the factory has the necessary skill sets and organization. So how does a factory become a universal supplier?

The Strategy

One would think that in the fashion garment industry the designer would be of primary importance. Yet this is not the case and, with the exception of the highest price designer labels, has not been the case for a very long time. Herein lies the advantage that opens the way for the universal factory supplier strategy.

In today's fashion industry, the designer plays only a minor role and then only at the outset of the design process. The actual process goes as follows:

   a. The designer, responsible for the initial design, who then passes the style on to the
   b. Technical designer, responsible for the fit and make, who adapts the shape of the original design as well as the look, who then passes the style on to the
   c. Overseas buying office merchandiser, responsible to ensure that the selected factory can actually produce the style (QA) and if not, who will change the style to fit the abilities of the factory, who then passes the style on to the
   d. Importer's department head who ensures that the style meets the target price and if not passes it back to the buying office merchandiser to make further changes.

The result is that the only person who actually cares about the look of the garment – the designer – is excluded from almost the entire design process. Under the circumstances we can understand why most designers purposely avoid looking at their garments in the store.

This reality leads to two serious problems:
   a. Increasingly garments sold by fashion retailers look like they were designed by a committee, most of whom know little about design.
   b. There is no one in the design process who can learn from the past – which garment sold and which did not sell – in order to use that knowledge in future designs.

The solution to this conundrum is to end design by committee and replace it with a partnership between the designer and their factory supplier.

The Guide to Cost-to-Value Analysis

The new process begins as follows:

a. The designer provides the first sketch.
b. The designer and the factory specialists confer back and forth to ensure that the factory understands what the designer requires.
c. When necessary, the factory sources the fabric which most closely follows the designer's original concept and at the same time has the necessary drape and feel to produce the garment closest to the designer's concept.
d. At every step along the way the designer/factory interplay continues, based on one basic criterion: THE DESIGNER OWNS THE DESIGN. Any necessary changes must be made by the designer.
    - If the selected fabric alters the garment look, the designer must change the design.
    - If the design cannot be produced in the factory, the designer must change the design.
    - If the garment cannot meet the target price, the designer must change the design.

The success of the strategy depends not only on the ability of the designer/factory partnership to provide a better garment, but more importantly for the designer, over a period of time, to create more saleable garments and where SALABILITY IS QUANTIFIABLE. The immediate goal is therefore not to sell more garments to the customer but rather to show the customer that the garments they buy from the factory are more salable. To accomplish this goal, two pieces of data are compiled:

- The hit rate: The percentage of confirmed orders from samples developed that come from the collaboration in design assists from the factory side.
- The sell through: The percentage of net profit derived from each style as a result of collaboration in design assists from the factory side.

The strategy succeeds because the designer learns from the data. For reasons, which frankly I cannot explain, once the designer takes responsibility for the design process and sees which of his/her designs are the better sellers, the designer will design garments that have a higher sell through which will automatically increase the hit rate.

The UNIVERSAL FACTORY SUPPLIER strategy described below addresses the problem of design integrity. To achieve it requires a hollowing out of the supply chain, where the role of the customer is limited to marketing and sales, with all other steps carried out between the customer's designer and the factory. While the designer is responsible for the design concept, all of the work must be carried out by the factory. The basic concept is illustrated in the diagram below.

Chapter 22   The Universal Factory Supplier

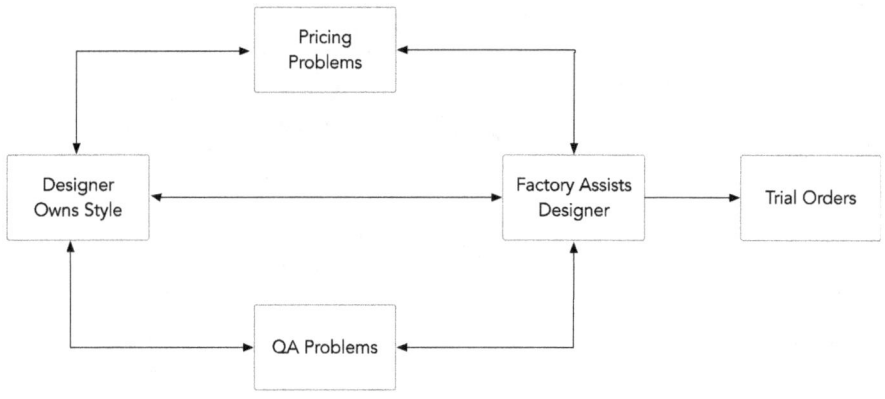

Universal Factory Supplier

To become a universal factory supplier, the parent factory must have the necessary structure and skill sets. The parent factory can be located anywhere in the world. But the parent factory must have a presence in close proximity to the customer, ideally a taxi ride's distance from the customer. For our purposes, let's say the customer is a major retailer with a large office located in Shanghai (although the customer can also be located anywhere). The parent factory must have its own wholly-owned presence in Shanghai in the form of a Shanghai-based factory branch office that acts as liaison between the parent factory and the customer. The customer also employs a full-time designer based in Shanghai.

Shanghai-based Factory Branch Office

The role of the Shanghai-based office is to act as a communication nexus between the parent factory and the customer and to ensure that the customer's designer's designs are produced satisfactorily. It does not have to be a large office: three or four people should be sufficient.

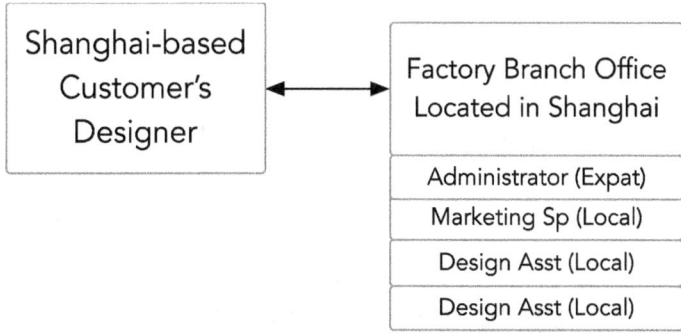

The Guide to Cost-to-Value Analysis

Shanghai Factory Branch Office Staff		
Title	Responsibilities	Description
Administrator	Signs checks, communicates with parent factory management	Expatriate sent from the parent factory to Shanghai branch office. Does not require technical knowledge
Marketing Specialist	Finds and develops new customers	Local Shanghai professional with good retailer connections
Design Assistant	Works with customer's designer	Local Shanghai professional and recent design school graduate. Able to cooperate (not compete) with customer's designer

The goal of the universal factory's Shanghai branch office is to support the customer, particularly the customer's in-house designer, and to help ensure the designer is successful.

The **design assistant** is the key Shanghai branch office player. It is their role to understand the designer's design and to ensure the parent factory's sample follows the designer's original concept. In this regard the factory's Shanghai branch office design assistant will travel between Shanghai and the parent factory on a regular basis. The **administrator** is someone from the parent company who holds the purse strings. The other parent company employee in Shanghai is a local **marketing specialist** who takes advantage of the set-up in Shanghai to look for new customers for the parent factory.

Modelista (master patternmaker)
This person is based back at the parent factory. The reality is that no one in the factory's Shanghai branch office nor the parent factory itself currently has the experience or skill sets to carry out the necessary steps to develop the required style. To achieve this strategy, it will be necessary to hire an experienced modelista who is the key player in the entire process.

Modelista	
Responsibilities	Description
<ul><li>Leads the entire process from first sketch to final sample approval;</li><li>Teaches those directly involved in the entire process to carry out their assigned tasks with a minimum of assistance</li></ul>	<ul><li>Expatriate (almost certainly European)</li><li>Master patternmaker</li><li>Experience working with designers and sample making</li><li>Experience running designer workshop</li></ul>

From the outset all information provided by the customer's designer is sent by the design assistant to the modelista. The modelista coaches the design assistant to obtain sufficiently rigorous information from the designer to allow the modelista to begin product development, while at the same time providing the designer with the information and material specifications necessary to correctly carry out the original design work.

Chapter 22 The Universal Factory Supplier

Changing Factory Support Structure

The effort and cost to create the universal factory supplier will be substantial. Much time and money can be saved by employing a professional to create and implement the model. Much also depends on ensuring that the new employees are qualified, experienced and knowledgeable. But the costs will be more than offset not only by introducing new customers to the factory but also by providing new and better services to existing customers.

In a sense, the universal factory supplier is the next development of the current highly successful transnational factory group. The difference is that while the transnational factory group requires replication of the factory for each new market, the universal factory requires only replication of the design and product development departments.

Traditional Factory Organization Structure

We think of a factory as an organization with two groups:

- The support departments, such as HR, admin, finance and shipping;
- The operational departments, such as design assist, merchandising, pattern making, sample making, QA, QC, and production.

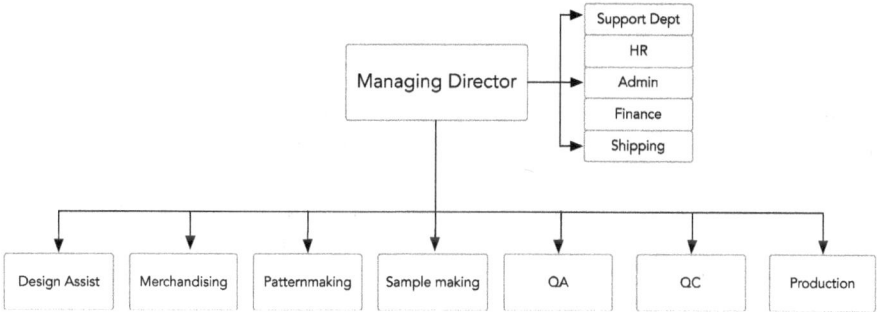

Universal Factory Supplier Structure

The universal factory supplier has a different structure. The support departments remain unchanged but the operational departments are no longer divided by different skills. Individual skills are brought together into a CUSTOMER CARE TEAM (located at the parent factory) whose sole purpose is to support the factory's Shanghai-based design assistant to meet the needs of the customer's designer.

The Guide to Cost-to-Value Analysis

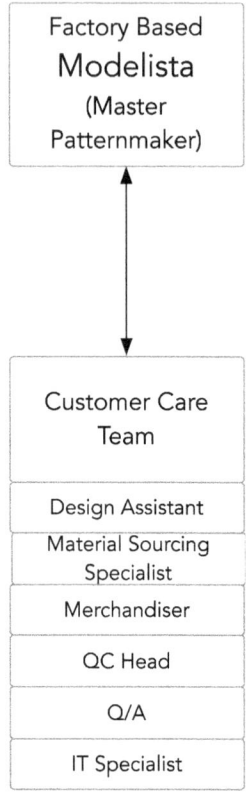

In a sense the entire focus of the universal factory supplier becomes customer-based. The responsibility of the customer care team is to be the customer's presence in the factory. At the outset this new structure will cause disruption because many people in the factory will believe that the members of the customer care team are no longer working for the factory. Instead they are working for the customer, fighting for faster delivery and even reduced FOB prices.

And, in a sense, they will be right. In fact, eventually as the members develop the necessary skill sets, the customer care team will become a semi-autonomous organization. Senior management will be able to give strategic instructions to each customer care team such as increased sales by 12% and net profit by 8% for the following year. As an added incentive, successful customer care teams are given bonuses when budgeted goals are exceeded. In the long run, the factory structure itself is fundamentally changed. Department by skill set is phased out and all work is carried out by customer care teams.

Chapter 23
Innovation

In a world where value is measured by gross profit, innovation invariably achieves the highest scores. Innovation by definition means there is no competition. If you have an innovative product, you are in a category by yourself and you are free to charge whatever the market will bear, regardless of your cost.

The greatest gross profit goes to DISRUPTIVE INNOVATION, something so original and so great that it destroys the existing market leaving that product or service as both the best thing in the market as well as the only thing in the market.

It is no wonder that companies everywhere have not only invested in innovation but also in ways to develop a culture of innovation. Some have gone further, making innovation not only a priority but an elite culture. These visionaries have set up centers of innovation throughout the developed world where they entice the world's most famous and highly educated specialists.

This leads to a fundamental question: How do you determine those with the talent for innovation? The answer depends on yet another question: What do you wish to innovate?

If you are Elon Musk working to invent the next generation spaceship, then the people most likely to bring you to the next generation are indeed the world's most famous and highly educated specialists. But if you are looking to create something less lofty such as the next Post-it note, then you have to look elsewhere if only because the great universities do not offer PhDs in stationery.

For those of us operating in the global garment and other small consumer product industries, our focus should be on the Post-it notes and not the next spaceship. All of which brings us back to the collaborative model, because the collaborative model is not exclusive, it is inclusive.

> Case Study XV: Pleated Skirts
>
> A factory producing high-quality women's silk garments for high-end designer labels receives a series of orders for engineered pleated printed silk skirts. Imagine a plaid design where each pleat must fall in the same place as the next pleat to ensure the horizontal lines match up. The problem is further exacerbated because due to the contoured nature of the waist seam, the precise width of each pleat will invariably be slightly different which means that to ensure that the vertical pattern repeat is maintained, no two pleats will be the exact same size. Now imagine that each skirt consists of 40 pleats and each pleat is sewn down seven inches from the waist.
>
> Fortunately the factory in question was organized into eight-person teams, each consisting of highly experienced multi-tasked sewers. Unfortunately producing 1000+ skirts would take each team over 120 days to complete, quite a bit more than the 10 working days scheduled.

The Guide to Cost-to-Value Analysis

> To make a long story short, one team came up with a solution which would reduce production time from 120 days to eight days, resulting in perfect skirts. Without going into details, it involved drilling holes in the fabric, a technique common to factories producing a $5 cotton flannel pajama for Kmart, certainly not $10/yard fabric for a skirt retailing for $500.
>
> The point is this was innovation of the Post-it note variety where the innovators were at best secondary school graduates but who knew everything there is to know about sewing silk garments. In our world, if you want a culture of innovation, you want to hear from everybody from senior management to the woman at the sewing machine.

We think of innovation in terms of new products. In fact, innovation can take multiple forms and each form is important:

- Innovation of materials
- Innovation of components
- Innovation of systems
- Innovation of products

> Case Study XVI: Component Innovation for Brushless Motors
>
> The chairman's limousine driver was an ardent model-building enthusiast. During a trip to the airport, the driver began talking to his passenger about his latest discovery concerning his favorite hobby, specifically the use of brushless motors.
>
> For model builders, the brushless motor enjoys several advantages over both the normal AC and DC motor:
>
> - More powerful
> - Longer lasting
> - Higher performance
> - Lighter weight
> - Less heat
>
> The chairman immediately recognized that the introduction of the brushless motor would solve a number of existing problems for several of his products. For example, hairdryers dry hair by employing a combination of heat and air. To achieve faster drying time most products at that time relied on greater temperature which unfortunately adversely affected the user's hair. The introduction of the brushless motor would increase the air flow, which would allow for a lower safer temperature, thus allowing faster and safer drying.
>
> Converting a brushless motor to use in a hair dryer required the efforts on the part of teams of specialists working both in China where the hair dryers were produced and in Japan where the motors were designed. It also required two years and millions of dollars.
>
> Once the new hair dryers went on sale, everyone did well making the effort and investment worthwhile. Yes, the new products would not have been possible without the work of teams of highly educated specialists, but on the other hand, these same highly educated specialists would have done nothing had it not been for the chairman's chauffeur and his interest in models.

Chapter 23 Innovation

Innovation is a four-step process:

1. Innovation Concept: the idea
2. Innovation Development: the plan for how that concept can become a product
3. Product Development: the workable product
4. Production: making the stuff

Case Study XVII: The Great Hair Cutter

We tend to think of innovation as an epiphany whereby the innovator receives a flash of understanding and to a large degree this is true. But we also believe that once the innovator has his flash, everything else follows smoothly and quickly. To a large degree this is not true.

The European head of an international personal care corporation had a great idea. He travelled to China to explain what he wanted. In Europe, men have to pay exorbitant sums for a simple haircut. The European head wanted to end this practice. He asked for an electric hair clipper that could be used at home with the following requirements:

a. The product should operate differently and be better than anything currently available in the market.
b. It should have a different look to anything available in the market.
c. It must have a competitive price.

The difference between the epiphany and the reality is similar to looking at a bird in flight and building a commercial jet. One step might follow the other but the real work occurs between the two.

As with many disruptive innovations, the do-it-yourself hair clipper took a considerable period of time to develop and, once developed, went through extensive iterations. But after nine years, sales are still going strong.

We are living in a world where innovation no longer belongs to an elite located in the industrialized world. The collaborative model relationship which includes the customer, the supplier and the consumer gives the most efficient and effective road to ongoing innovation.

Chapter 24
The Customer Side

For decades, retailer and brand customers have been aware of value-added services available from the supplier side. The question is, why have they been unwilling to take advantage of these services? What are the obstacles?

Many customers appear to be trapped in the distant past, blindly following the competitive model where FOB price determines which factory should get the order. For the most part, senior executives on the customer side still think of the supplier side as something of secondary importance and product sourcing as a support unit with the sole purpose to ensure that things run smoothly and that low FOB prices are achieved.

The first problem is systemic – poor cost analysis whereby senior executives running multibillion-dollar retail and brand operations have little or no idea of actual product costs. They do not understand the potential role of the factory. Consequently they do not include the benefits of cost-reducing services, such as moving product development from the customer to the factory or the ability of the factory to reduce markdowns, because neither product development nor markdowns are listed in the cost sheet.

The second problem is structural, whereby the customer's management culture restricts the customer's ability to accept value-added services from the factory.

- Senior management has no understanding of the relationship between their role as the customer and that of the supplier and therefore rely entirely on their subordinates.
- Those middle managers have no interest in change, regardless of the benefits to their company (see case study below).
- Those on the customer side who directly interact with the suppliers are for the most part still committed to the FOB-price-above-all competitive strategy.

Case Study XVIII: Unwanted Service

You are head of logistics for Schmidlap Stores. You are responsible for all inward shipping, customs clearance, distribution and local delivery to Schmidlap Stores' 1200 branches. You operate five distribution centers. Your department employs 850 staff and 16 executives. Last year you earned $475,000 including bonus. You have a daughter at university and a son in drug rehab. Including your mortgage, you have debts totalling $1.8 million. In short, you are the normal successful corporate executive. You are broke!

The Guide to Cost-to-Value Analysis

> One early Monday morning the CEO calls you into his office. "Ed, I have received an interesting offer from one of our major suppliers, Schmata Knitters. Mr. Wong suggests that in future, his factory will provide complete door-to-door service for all his shipments. Schmata will ship, clear the goods, break down the order by store and deliver directly to every branch. I think this is a good idea. If this works out we can reduce staff, close down our distribution centers and get rid of those annoying truckers. Schmata is a reliable company and Mr. Wong strikes me as a serious person. What do you think?"
>
> You can give two possible answers:
> 1. "*I think this is a great idea. This will save Schmidlap Stores a pile of money, simplify our critical path and reduce our risk by making the supplier responsible for the entire logistics process. If Schmata performs as we both hope, we can encourage our other major suppliers to follow suit and within 18 months my department will be 100% superfluous. I think we should begin downsizing my department at once.*"
>
> 2. "*What – are you some sort of nutcase? Absolutely not! Who is this Wong character and what does he know about logistics? And as far as Schmidlap Stores is concerned, do you really think that some t-shirt factory in Phnom Penh can run logistics in the U.S.? I can assure you that if you allow Wong to move a single t-shirt independently of my department, not only will Schmata be out of business within a year, but so too will Schmidlap Stores.*"
>
> Which answer would you select? Let me give you a hint. Since the first Pleistocene garmento left his cave to sell used sabre-tooth tiger skins to his Neanderthal neighbors, no one has ever opted for answer #1.

There was a time when the expression "moving at a glacial pace" was meant to describe the slowest progress imaginable. Yet here we are operating in a world where the glaciers are moving backwards faster than our industry is moving forward. I ask you, what kind of revolution is that?

Think about this: In 1975, Inditex instituted speed-to-market which made Zara the largest and most successful garment retailer in the world. Here we are 44 years later still debating if speed-to-market is the way to go. What are we waiting for?

Think about this: In the early 1970s, Hong Kong-based factories were providing complete product development – from receipt of designer sketch to sample approval – all within a period of less than 30 days. Yet here we are, in 2020, still asking whether the transfer of product development to the factories is at all possible.

As we can see from the above, customers fail because in an ever-changing industry, they have trapped themselves in a culture and system that severely limits their ability to both create and accept change. Fortunately some years ago a new generation of better educated, more flexible sourcing professionals began to recognize and accept that factory value-added services were able to bring substantial benefit to

Chapter 24 The Customer Side

their companies. These sourcing professionals went so far as to provide their more important suppliers with engineers and other specialists to train these factories with the skill sets necessary to perform the services. Thus was born the cooperative model.

The industry is now entering a new collaborative model. While the older competitive and cooperative models were based on cost reduction, this new model is based on innovation, whereby the customer and its factory supplier, working in partnership, can accomplish things previously thought to be impossible. Herein lies the problem.

Over time factories have evolved from simple product makers to sophisticated service providers. The sourcing specialists and their teams have evolved from simple order givers to sophisticated skill-set developers. Together both sides have learned to work in tandem to provide increased value to the customer which senior executives at some retail and brand operations have acknowledged and have grown to rely on.

Unfortunately, many of those at the very top of the customer's senior management pyramid still cannot accept the factory supplier as a partner in the supply chain. Senior management continues to consider the relationship between the customer and the factory supplier at best as an important support operation where the role of the supply chain head is limited to ensuring that bad things do not happen. The supply chain head is not expected to make strategic decisions that might affect the company itself.

As we will see in the next chapters, the innovations which become possible with the collaborative model can only move forward in a true partnership relationship, where the factory supplier is willing and able to make the necessary commitments of time and money because of irrevocable guarantees by the customer.

Chapter 25
The Space-Time Continuum

We recognize that in our industry, everything comes down to cost. We also recognize that to a large degree cost is directly related to time.

- Reduced product development lead time reduces cost by bringing the style to market when demand is greatest.
- Fast-turn production reduces cost by allowing for trial orders.
- Quick response reduces costs by allowing for re-orders of the bestselling styles.
- Speed-to-market reduces costs by reducing markdowns.

What is not so obvious is that our entire industry operates in the dimension of time where every single link in the supply chain is time-sensitive. The real supply chain consists of literally thousands of steps. Let's look at a lowly zipper, the simplest part of the process and show just how a zipper relates to time.

If a zipper is required to produce a garment it must be included in the supply chain. The zipper-buying process usually begins when the factory receives the customer's color/quantity breakdown. At that point the factory contacts the local YKK agent (one day) who quotes a unit price ($0.10) and confirms the order. The local YKK agent takes the zippers out of stock and sends them to the factory (three days). The factory receives the zippers and inspects them – the customer has given the factory the right to approve trims – at which point the process is complete. Cost: $0.10 per zipper and four days.

Zipper available locally and factory can approve: 4 days

Color Quantity Breakdown Received	Zippers Ordered (1) ($0.10)	Zippers Received (3)	Zippers Inspected Ready for Production 4 ($0.10)

Unfortunately anyone who has ever worked in a garment factory knows that life is not always so straightforward. For example, let's say the factory is in the Dominican Republic. As before, the factory receives the color/quantity breakdown and contacts the local YKK agent to order the zippers. But instead of receiving the zippers, the factory is advised that one of the colors required is not in stock. The local agent must go to the YKK regional office which is in another country to obtain the zippers of that color.

No problem. The factory has lost only four days. If the factory is lucky, the regional YKK office has everything they need – order processing, shipping, custom's clearance and local transportation now adds another 12 days bringing the total time to 16 days. But if the factory is notified that the regional office also doesn't have what they need, the order must now be sent to the nearest YKK factory. There is a second delay of 21 days production time.

The factory now has a real problem. The good news is that the zipper that once cost 10¢ still costs 10¢. The bad news is that the zipper that once required four days, then 16 days, now requires 37 days including shipping, custom's clearance and local delivery time.

The Guide to Cost-to-Value Analysis

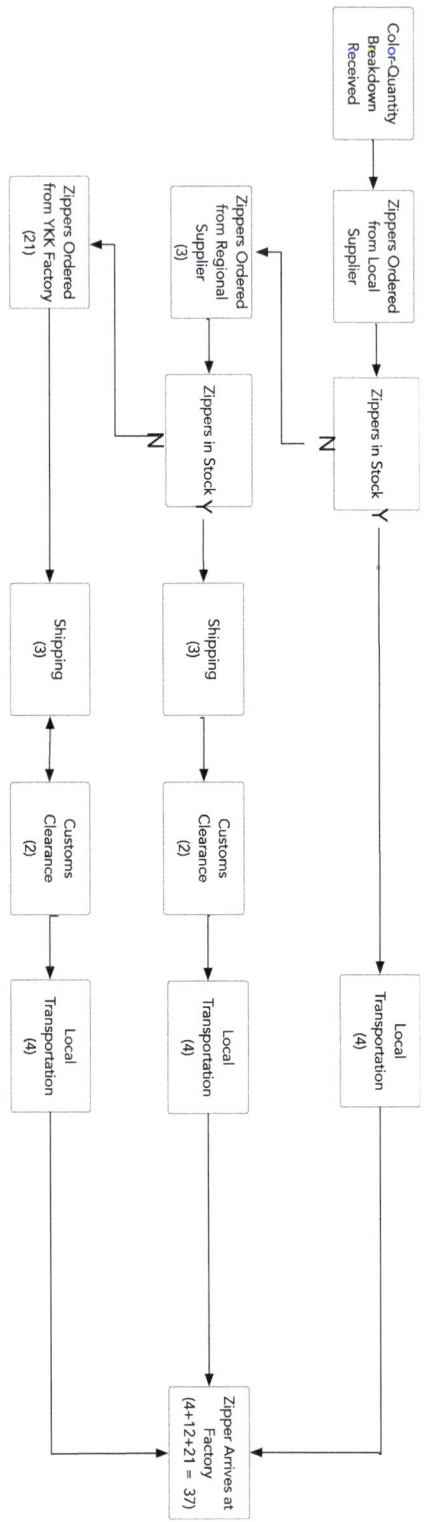

130

Chapter 25 The Space-Time Continuum

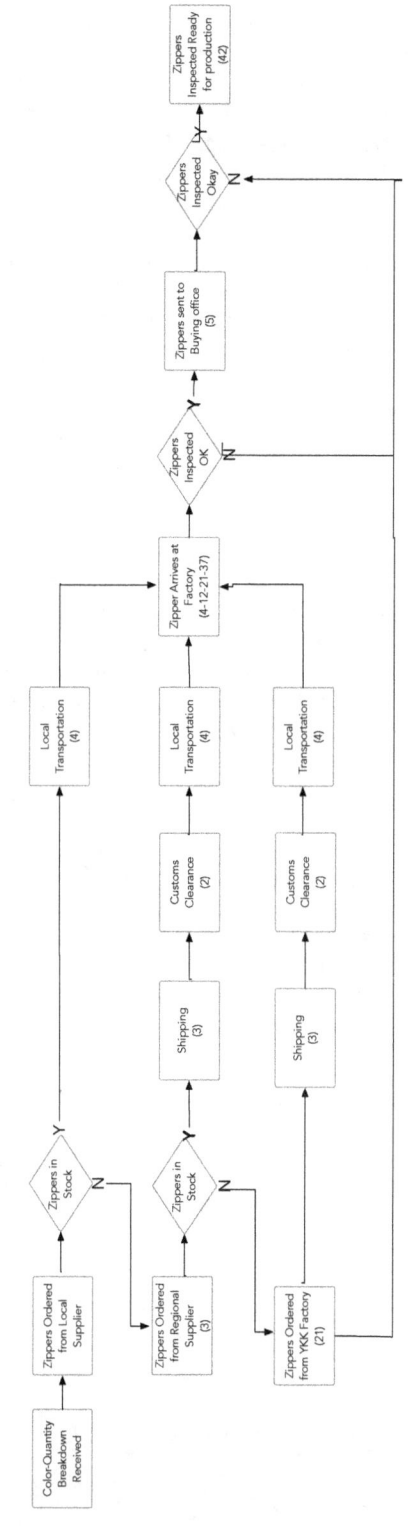

The Guide to Cost-to-Value Analysis

The flow chart on the previous page illustrates the worst-case scenario. This happens when the factory does not have the right to approve the zipper. First of all, the customer's buying office inspection adds a further five days to the process bringing the total to 42 days. If the customer's buying office fails the zipper, things could get as bad as 72+ days with a further 21 days for production and more shipment, custom's clearance and local transportation time as well as another five days for the second inspection. This clearly becomes a nightmare.

Zipper rejection may be infrequent but can occur from a variety of reasons:

- The factory ordered the wrong zipper.
- The factory ordered the right zipper but their YKK color card may have been old and faded.
- The factory ordered the right zipper and they had a new color card but the YKK zipper produced was of a slightly different hue.

The solution to the frustrating scenario described above lies within the supply chain, provided the supply chain includes the extended flow chart shown above. Once we recognize the degree to which time can affect costs, we can take steps to obviate the risks. Usually the customer (through his buying office or agent) designates the zipper supplier leaving the factory to actually order the zippers from the designated zipper supplier and therein creates the potential problem. **If the buying office/agent middleman both designates and also physically orders the zippers, the problem would disappear and potential lead time delays would be eliminated.**

In the old way of working, the factory can enter the process only after it receives the COLOR/QUANTITY BREAKDOWN. But if we examine the supply chain flow chart particularly at the early stages of product development, we can see that the COLOR STANDARDS covering all styles for the period are available long before anyone decides which factory will produce which orders and often even before the actual garment design work has been completed. Consequently there is substantial free time between COLOR STANDARDS and the COLOR/QUANTITY BREAKDOWN. Preproduction work on zippers could be carried out to ensure the color is correct even before the style has been designed and the possibility of mistakes occurring would be reduced.

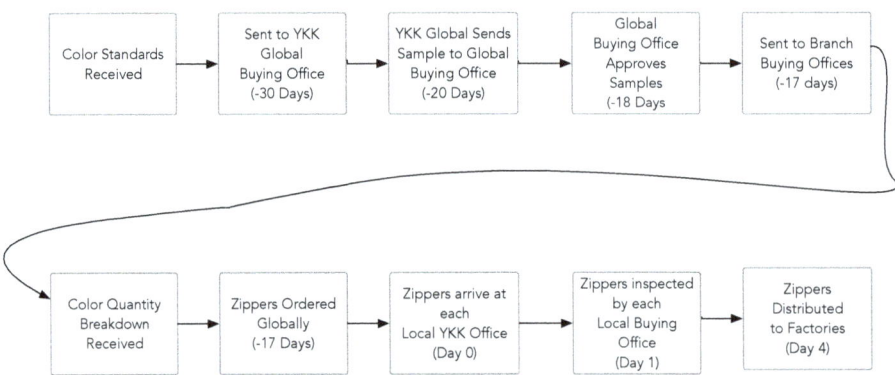

Customer's buying office/agent orders zippers: 4 days

Chapter 25 The Space-Time Continuum

A major importer might place 10,000 orders per month from perhaps 50 factories located in five countries. Assuming 25% to be skirts or pants, zippers are required for 2500 orders. Assuming the bottoms in each color come in four colors, not necessarily the same colors for each order, it is not unreasonable to expect the aggregate 50 factories to place orders of 10000 pieces of zippers per color monthly. If even 1% of the 2500 orders have problems, then 25 orders per month will be shipped late which would be hugely disruptive.

When the buying office/agent takes over the responsibility of ordering the zippers, the 50 zipper buyers located in five countries is reduced to one zipper buyer located in one country, who then arranges with YKK to divide the order among the five countries producing goods. The 2500 zipper orders are reduced to one or two orders (depending on whether a 6" zipper and a 7" zipper is counted as one or two orders). The four colors could be expanded to include all 50+ colors in YKK's color standard.

The steps for having the buying office/agent order the zippers are as follows:

1. During estimated 30 days of free time (FT) before factory receives any color/quantity data:
    a. Color standards arrive at the buying office/agent (FT Day -30)
    b. Buying office/agent visits YKK Global (FT Day -30)
        i. Colors available on the YKK color card are selected and approved
        ii. Colors not available on color card are developed by YKK (FT Day -20)
    c. All colors approved by buying office/agent (FT Day -18)
    d. Approved samples sent to branch buying office (FT Day -17)

2. Supply chain lead times
    a. Color/quantity breakdown received
    b. Zippers ordered by buying office/agent for all factories worldwide
    (FT Day -17)
    c. Zippers arrive at local YKK suppliers (FT Day 0)
    d. Zippers inspected by local middleman office (one day)
    e. Zippers arrive at designated factory (three days)

The move from factory zipper-ordering to middleman zipper-ordering will greatly reduce the number of mistakes. It will also make everybody's job – customer, middleman, factory and YKK – easier and in doing so reduce everybody's cost. Unfortunately no system is perfect. There will be fewer mistakes but there will still be mistakes. In this regard, the greatest benefit of this change will be more efficient use of time allowing any mistakes to be rectified before they create delays.

The Guide to Cost-to-Value Analysis

YKK is an excellent zipper supplier that makes the greatest effort to ensure customer satisfaction. Nevertheless, we all must live in the real world and in this real world the buying service that is responsible for annual garment exports of $1+ billion has more clout and receives better support than a 200-machine factory in the Dominican Republic.

A final note. I admit this has not been the world's most exciting chapter. If you have made it thus far, either you are a most conscientious professional or, more likely, you have been involved in one or more zipper disasters.

BOOK III
The Way Forward
or
The Future is Now

Chapter 26
Evolutionary Changes

We think of great change as revolutionary. We speak of Creative Destruction and Disruptive Innovation. In fact, we think of every change as revolutionary and every week seems to bring its own revolution. These changes are undeniably important, or at least of potential importance. We talk about internet and e-commerce, digitization, big data, AI, reshoring, 3D pattern making, robotic machinery. The list is endless and each change is indeed important. Nevertheless, we also have to accept that while the technology is revolutionary, its effect on the industry may be significantly less and, in some cases, non-existent.

The same industries that speak glibly of the revolutionary technology that will replace workers with machines fail to recognize that better training and better treatment of their workers might lead to higher productivity at substantially lower cost (see Chapter 3 Intrinsic Cost Savings). At the same time, many customers who have jumped on the CSR bandwagon still paradoxically base their sourcing decisions on CM price. Services which have proved effective for the past 40 years, such as speed-to-market and moving product development from the customer's home country to the supplier are still being debated.

In our world where, THE MORE THINGS CHANGE THE MORE THEY REMAIN THE SAME, how do we denote change beyond revolution? I suggest we move from revolutionary to evolutionary. If we think of our industry players and their relationships with one another, what is happening in our industry at this very moment can be described as mass extinction. Twenty years down the line, what we define now as factories, brands and retailers may have totally disappeared and the relationship among the new sectors will be entirely different.

Horizontal Integration

The original players were the factory, the brand wholesaler and the retailer. Historically, the brand was at the center of the process. The brand developed the product. The brand sourced the factories that made the products. The brand wholesaled the product to the retailer who went on to sell the product to the consumer. This was an extremely costly and not particularly efficient way of doing business.

Look at the numbers for a garment which begins at FOB $8.00:

- $10.20: Landed delivery-duty-paid (DDP)
- $12.46: 55% wholesale markup
- $22.66: Wholesale price charged to the retailer
- $67.97: 75% Retailer markup
- $90.63: Retail Price = 11 times FOB price
- $31.72: Markdown 35%
- $58.91: Net Retail Price
- $36.25: Net Retailer Profit 40%

The Guide to Cost-to-Value Analysis

Retailer Buys from Brand Wholesaler		
FOB Price		$8.00
Agent Commission	5.0%	$0.40
Freight		$0.25
Duty	16.2%	$1.30
Clearance		$0.10
Local Transport		$0.15
DDP		$10.20
Wholesale Markup	55.0%	$12.46
Wholesale Price		$22.66
Retail Markup	75.0%	$67.97
Retail Price		$90.63
Markdown	35.0%	$31.72
Net Retail Price		$58.91
Net Retailer Profit		$36.25

Over time, the traditional model began to fall apart and the first evolutionary change took place. When the price on the hangtag approached 10 times FOB price, both the retailers and the wholesale brands decided change was necessary, albeit with different motivations. The retailers changed the rules. Their new policy was to force the brands to guarantee a maximum markdown rate, whereby if the markdown exceeded a given percentage, the brand would be held responsible and required to repay the retailer.

Change didn't stop there. The next step for the retailers was to cut out the wholesaler brand completely by creating house labels and going FACTORY DIRECT. The retailer moved sourcing in-house and began working directly with the factories. This was the era when Gap became the largest garment retailer in the U.S.

On the other side, the brands began to move to RETAIL DIRECT by opening their own stores. For years the large, more successful brands followed a two-prong strategy. First their stores were dedicated, selling only their own brand and avoiding in-house competition from other brands. Then they reduced their selling prices by combining their wholesale and retail markups into a single retail markup. By removing links in the previous supply chain, horizontal integration was taking place.

The former advantages of the wholesale brand's role disappeared. Where once wholesale was a risk-free process where the brand's responsibility ended the minute they shipped the order to the retailer, they were now required to take the

Chapter 26 Evolutionary Changes

risk that the consumer might not actually by the stuff. Why take the risk if there is no share in the profit?

Of course, the smaller brands still remained trapped as before because they could not afford the cost of opening their own stores, just as the small retailers remained trapped because their quantities were too small and their knowledge too little to source garments on their own. But for the big players on both sides cutting each other out proved to be extremely profitable, with both showing substantial increases in new profit with massive markups when they were able to maintain their original retail prices.

Retailer Buys Factory Direct		
FOB		$8.00
Agent Commission	5.0%	$0.40
Freight		$0.25
Duty	16.2%	$1.30
Clearance		$0.10
Local Transport		$0.15
DDP		$10.20
Product Development	20.0%	$2.04
Wholesale Price		$12.24
Retail Markup	86.5%	$78.39
Retail Price		$90.63
Markdown	35.0%	$31.72
Net Retail		$58.91
Net Customer Profit		$46.67

Wholesaler Brand Goes Retail Direct		
FOB		$8.00
Agent Commission	5.0%	$0.40
Freight		$0.25
Duty	16.2%	$1.30
Clearance		$0.10
Local Transport		$0.15
DDP		$10.20
Product Development		N/A
Wholesale Price		$10.20
Retail Markup	88.7%	$80.43
Retail Price		$90.63
Markdown	35.0%	$31.72
Net Retail		$58.91
Net Customer Profit		$48.71

But internet and the resulting e-commerce dramatically changed everything. With internet, all brands automatically became global companies. The marketplace had now opened to both big and small companies. The old costing where an FOB $8.00 garment would retail for over $90.00 was out the window, replaced by the same garment retailing for only $41.50, less than half.

The Guide to Cost-to-Value Analysis

Brand Retails via Internet Provider		
FOB		$8.00
Agent Commission	5.0%	$0.40
Freight		$0.25
Duty	16.2%	$1.30
Clearance		$0.10
Local Transport		$0.15
DDP		$10.20
Product Development	20.0%	$2.04
Wholesale Price		$12.24
Internet Provider	5.0%	$2.07
Retail Markup	55.0%	$27.19
Retail Price		$41.49
Markdown	35.0%	$14.52
Net Retail		$26.97
Net Customer Profit		$14.74

As e-commerce developed, a new middleman – the internet provider – came into existence. Where once the brand was on its own, hoping to develop customers through word-of-mouth and social media, they could now become part of major online retailers such as Etsy or Amazon, companies with hundreds of millions of followers.

That was the past. Here is a possible future. In this new world, the previous three-legged animal will become extinct, replaced with a single provider: the factory/brand/retailer. This evolutionary change is again the Collaborative Model, a universal relationship where competitors work together to achieve common goals involving all players both inside – suppliers and their customers – and outside the industry – NGOs, labor organizations, development banks and governments.

Parallax is an astronomical term describing the degree to which the position of an object appears to change because of the real change of the position of the observer. Two observers seeing the same object from different positions would perceive that object differently. The greater the difference in their positions, the greater the difference in their perceptions. What is true of the universe at large is equally true of the garment industry.

Within the industry itself, there exist two perceptions, between which there is a gap resulting from parallax. There are those who still live in an unchanging past, who have learned nothing, forgotten nothing and who are therefore doomed to

Chapter 26 Evolutionary Changes

repeat the same mistakes over and over again. Under these conditions progress is very slow.

But things have finally begun to change. New entrants to the industry are better educated and, dare I say, smarter than those of us who came before. They understand and therefore do not fear technological change. Through their efforts, not only are customers and their factory suppliers working together, but competitors have discovered the advantages of creating *modus vivendi* to work together in areas where interests coincide. The parallax gap between the old and the new industries is gradually closing and will hopefully disappear as the most incompetent of the old industry die off.

There is yet a second parallax gap between the industry itself and the outside institutional world. To the institutional garment world, the garment industry is the indispensable first step to industrial development as well as the entry into world trade. To many developing and least developed countries, the garment industry is both the largest industrial employer as well as the largest provider of foreign exchange. In some countries, the garment industry is the only industrial employer and, with the exception of remittances from overseas workers, the only source of foreign exchange.

From the institutional point of view, the garment industry is rapidly becoming the most important tool to analyze social, political and economic development. To sociologists, the garment industry offers the socio-economic tool equivalent to the Big Mac currency index. Where else but in the garment industry do you find literally tens of thousands of factories located in every country in the world producing identical products from identical raw materials? This standardization allows sociologists and cultural anthropologists to understand the degree to which societies and cultures foster or restrict industrial development.

To economists, the garment industry is the industrial equivalent of Fra Mendel's fruit flies. Companies in other industries may design, produce and market 5, 50 or even 100 models a year. In the garment industry, some garment factories will produce 1000 models a month and some fashion brand importers and retailers may market literally 100,000 models a year. In this sense, the global garment industry has not only become the key to economic development but, equally importantly, the key to understanding the mechanics of economic development.

To the garmento world, the garment industry is the highest risk, most competitive and most chaotic industry in the world. If the garmento does not think long term, it is because the garment industry has no long term. Two back-to-back bad seasons and a company that may have been in business for 30 years is gone, disappeared. Second only to mediocre Italian restaurants, the garment industry has the highest rate of attrition in the industrialized world.

There are perhaps 250,000 garment export factories worldwide. (No one knows how many there are – the number grows every second). They are chasing

The Guide to Cost-to-Value Analysis

approximately 25,000 importers/retailers. (No one knows how many there are – the number shrinks every second). About 50 importers account for 60% of all U.S. garment imports and approximately the same holds true in the EU. On the supplier side, the industry is consolidating to the point where within a decade, 50 transnational factories worldwide will account for 50% of all garment exports. The industry is moving so quickly that fashion no longer evolves. Rather items appear, dominate sales for a matter of weeks, only to disappear, leaving those unable to move fast enough with mounds of last week's style of unsold and now totally unsaleable merchandise. In the world of the garmento, the expression goes, "Here today, gone today."

The industry has its own insane paradigms. The sane people, who manufacture cigarettes, drugs, automobiles and other weapons of mass destruction, may speak of increasing quality and efficiency by reducing damages and cutting out unnecessary operations. In the fashion industry we do just the opposite. We work with damaged materials such as distressed denim and raw-edged dresses. We add unnecessary operations such as pleats, pin tucks, darts, gussets, and burnt-out embroidery.

The institutional garment and garmento worlds are indeed different. However, it is not their different perceptions of the global garment industry that should concern us, but rather their almost identical perceptions of each other. The most benign assessment of their relationship is that there is no relationship. At best, each assiduously ignores the other. At worst, regrettably, indifference is often replaced by visceral abhorrence and contempt.

For years, the institutional garment world looked at those who worked in the garmento world as uneducated, irresponsible and greedy dolts who neither knew nor cared to know how they impact the countries in which they work. NGOs and the International Labor Organization (ILO) were convinced that without constant oversight by the compliance police, greedy factory owners would invariably revert to their Mr. Hyde personae. They would employ ten-year-old children to work 60-hour weeks in sweatshop conditions. Sexual harassment would once again become endemic. Wages would fall below the minimum required for subsistence. Garmento executives were perceived to have no real qualifications, merely substituting peasant cunning for real intelligence and relying entirely on personal experience. The garmentos followed no industry standard because the garment industry had no industry standard. For the institutional garment world, decisions in the garmento world are made solely for short-term advantage.

The garmento world looked at its institutional twin in much the same way, as a bunch of overeducated, irresponsible egomaniacs who have allowed self-indulgence to override common sense. They thought those in the institutional world lived inside ivy-covered towers totally isolated from reality, where their practical knowledge of the global garment industry extended only as far as the aisles of Saks Fifth Avenue. Garmentos thought that those who work in NGOs and the ILO assume that the sole reason for the existence of garment factories

Chapter 26 Evolutionary Changes

is to give substance to the latest crackpot schemes of those institutions. The garmentos were convinced that the institutions could think long term only because they have no understanding of what goes on from Monday to Sunday in the real world.

These prejudices notwithstanding, the perceptions the two worlds held of each other were actually reasonably accurate. More importantly, their seemingly conflicting perceptions of the garment industry itself were also essentially accurate, just incomplete. Together, the two worlds have a complete understanding of the global garment industry. But taken separately, the perception of each is fundamentally and dangerously flawed.

Most of the truly catastrophic events in the history of the garment industry can be traced back to the failure of the garmentos and institutions to cooperate with one another. The garmento side was certainly responsible for many of these disasters. The high tariff walls, the quota regime, the lunatic rules of origin which distorted the international garment trade between 1963 and 2004, were all the direct result of the naïve belief on the part of the garmentos that a closed market would ensure their success.

In the case of the U.S., these restrictions ultimately resulted in the demise of both the local garment makers and their domestic fabric suppliers. All this might have been avoided had the garmentos sought the advice and help of trained economists. They might have learned that what held true in 301ce, when the Emperor Diocletian imposed the first textile import quotas, holds true today – blanket protectionism more often than not is a form of suicide by bankruptcy.

Those on the institutional side caused more than their fair share of mischief. The 2005 quota phase-out, which eventually resulted in the loss of literally millions of jobs in the least developed countries, was, to a large degree, the result of lobbying by NGOs and international institutions who – either through ignorance or negligence – convinced their client countries that a free market would increase their exports. Any Seventh Avenue importer could have told them that China would be the big winner in any quota phase-out.

Fortunately, we have the beginning of a new relationship, between the world of the garmentos and the world of the institutions, which if successful will close the parallax gap once and for all and allow for cooperative relationships. This is the essence of the Collaborative Model.

Chapter 27
The Collaborative Model: Part II

As these things are usually measured, the global garment industry is not particularly large. In fact, global garment exports are slightly smaller than Walmart annual sales. But in other respects, the garment industry is indeed of global importance.

- It is probably the world's second largest employer, after subsistence agriculture.
- It operates in some of the world's poorest countries.
- Its employees are predominantly women.
- It is a first step of industrial development, in many cases the largest industry in the country, and in some cases the only industry in the country.
- It is often the greatest source of foreign exchange.

Unfortunately the industry has often not played a constructive role in the countries where it operates. Many of the complaints listed by governments, NGOs and international institutions are valid. In some countries, low wages, excessive overtime, poor working conditions and pollution created by the industry are endemic.

On the other hand, conditions in other countries are not only better but improving. We forget that many of the economic development "winners" such as China, South Korea, Hong Kong and more recently, Vietnam, started their rise with the garment industry.

It is difficult for professionals, let alone the general population, to understand what is going on. The state of the global garment industry and its problems are complex. Much of the so-called data available on the internet is deeply flawed and extremely unreliable. Contrary to common belief, garment production is not a major contributor to global warming nor are poor working conditions limited to poor countries. Although poor compliance is certainly more common in poor countries, its existence in wealthy countries is more reprehensible.

The good news is that an increasing number of both customers and suppliers are working to improve conditions, many with notable success. There is a growing move to industry-wide organizations to deal with the problems on the supplier front. The Rana Plaza catastrophe brought about two industry organization to improve safety conditions in Bangladesh factories: the U.S.-led Bangladesh Alliance for Worker Safety and the EU-led Accord on Fire and Building Safety in Bangladesh. Both organizations, funded by their respective industries, have shown excellent tangible results and will serve as models going forward.

At the same time, the regional development banks, the World Bank and other

The Guide to Cost-to-Value Analysis

development organizations have a mixed record. All too often, the result of their efforts is a 100-page report that moves seamlessly from a crisp presentation at an international symposium to a moldering future in some forgotten file cabinet.

On the plus side their work in social overhead capital is commendable. Without decent roads, electricity and professional education, industrial development is impossible. These are indeed prerequisites for development. The problem is that while they are necessary for development to take place, social overhead capital does not directly translate to industrial development.

To move forward there must be a way to relate development bank investment and loans to employment. How many jobs can we expect to be created from the funds? This requires collaboration between the banks and the industry. Unfortunately for many years the garment industry and the development organizations have been in conflict. But there are examples where industry and institutions have joined together in a Collaborative Model to positive results. Here are two of them.

Hawassa

The story begins in 2014 when an informal group of major customers started talking about a new sourcing strategy. They were concerned that with a market share by volume in excess of 40%, China had become too-much-of-a-good-thing. The immediate question was, where else could customers go?

At that time, Myanmar was just opening up. This was the last of the great (or potentially great) Asian garment-exporting countries. Myanmar looked pretty good. It was home to an existing industry, with a pool of well-trained workers, producing complex fashion goods. There was no need to begin with cheap commodities. The customer could order dresses, suits and overcoats from the first order. Better still, Myanmar is located in the same neighborhood as other major Asian garment-exporting countries. There was no need to set up a new buying office. Customers could begin with a small branch office.

But fresh in customers' minds were Bangladesh's Tazreen and Rana Plaza factory disasters and the nasty fights over working conditions and workers' rights which were (and still are) endemic in South and Southeast Asia. From this came the conclusion that building a national industry from the ground up might be a sound investment. After all, consumers were becoming aware of the need for corporate social responsibility (CSR) and rather than forcing change on unwilling exporting countries, it might be easier to start an industry with high CSR standards from the get-go.

This would be a long-term, difficult and expensive project. The customers needed a country where the long-term value was appreciably higher than the long-term costs. At this point major customer Philip Van Heusen (PVH) stepped in and became the project leader. The immediate conclusion was Africa. It was

Chapter 27   The Collaborative Model: Part II

logistically easier than South America, the only other possible location. After more detailed research, the decision was made to build the new industry in Ethiopia.

Ethiopia had many problems. It was one of the world's poorest countries. It had no garment industry and for that matter very little industry at all. The population, for the most part, survives on subsistence agriculture. The country is landlocked, the road network non-existent. At the time, the cost of moving a container from a factory to the nearest port in Djibouti was in excess on $10,000. Very early the World Bank joined the project[1] which eventually resulted in the Hawassa Industrial Park.

Hawassa is located 285kms south of the capital Addis Ababa. By second quarter 2019, 23 manufacturers, most with foreign joint venture partners, were operating or had signed MOUs to operate in the park. Almost from the outset, the project had many problems which exacerbated over time. These problems came to the public eye when in May 2019, The Stern Center for Business and Human Rights (New York University) published a serious critique of the Hawassa Project[2].

Stern Report

The report was called 'Made in Ethiopia: Challenges in the Garment Industry's New Frontier'. The authors argued that the investments of PVH and its collaborators in Hawassa were motivated by low wages. Absent from the report were the efforts to create a better industry and no mention of the benefits of cheap electricity.

The authors' conclusions were implacable. The report goes on to suggest that most of the problems at Hawassa are the direct result of low wages, including worker dissatisfaction, 100% worker attrition and wide-scale industrial action.

The problems described in the report are indeed serious. But I am concerned that important facts, unique to the garment industry, were overlooked. This has resulted in an incomplete analysis that disregards fundamental characteristics of what PVH and industry players are attempting to do.

To start at the beginning: Why did PVH and the other players go to Hawassa in the first place? I suggest that the report's accusation that PVH was motivated by cheap labor is totally incorrect. PVH is well known throughout the industry for their outstanding ethical record. In this regard, everyone in the industry is

---

1   http://documents.worldbank.org/curated/en/163511499673766520/pdf/117302-WP-PUBLIC-PVHCaseStudythJuneHRsingles.pdf
    http://documents.worldbank.org/curated/en/573211562218693613/pdf/Ethiopia-Estimating-the-Impact-of-the-Mojo-Hawassa-Expressway.pdf
2   https://issuu.com/nyusterncenterforbusinessandhumanri/docs/nyu_ethiopia_final_online

The Guide to Cost-to-Value Analysis

aware of their efforts to build an industry in Ethiopia based on compliance, sustainability and transparency.

The issue of cheap electricity is a prime consideration within the industry. It is understandable that because the Stern Report's authors have limited knowledge of the industry, they are unaware of PVH's reputation or plan, as well as the crucial importance of electricity in both the textile and garment production processes. Even so, you don't have to be an industry expert to realize that if you have a designer label business, your greatest asset is your label. The idea that PVH management would be so incredibly incompetent as to jeopardize their label's reputation to save 20¢ on CM is unfathomable.

The matter of wages is equally serious. The information provided in the Stern Report on wages is more than likely accurate and of great value. The problem is how the report deals with the information. The average sewer at Hawassa is paid about $50 a month, while the same sewer working at a legitimate factory located in New York City is paid literally 50 times more or $2500. If you are sitting in Washington Square Park in New York City the wage disparity would seem to be totally unconscionable. But if you are sitting in Gullele Park in Addis Ababa, your perspective would be different. Where an educated government clerk is paid $21 a month and the same clerk working in a bank or insurance company office is paid $18 a month, $50 a month paid to women aged 18-25 and more than likely illiterate might be considered equally unconscionable, but from the other direction.

In a real sense, the question is less about the sewer's income and more about her expenditure. As pointed out in the report, the cost of living at Hawassa including housing, food and other necessities was so high that the sewer had little or no money at the end of the month. Any garment professional who has experience building factories in least developed countries where the economy is based on subsistence farming knows that to succeed the factory must look after its workers. The factory must ensure that at the end of each month, the worker is able to send fully half of their total wage to their family. This might mean subsidized housing and food but this is a requirement if the factory wants to keep its workers. Furthermore, at the end of the day, it matters less what the worker is paid and more what benefit the worker achieves from his or her work.

Then there is the matter of 100% worker attrition cited in the report. I am sure the authors are not suggesting that on Monday 25,000 people showed up to work and Tuesday zero people showed up. I assume that their figure of 100% attrition is based on the monthly loss over a period of time. While there are many areas of discussion over problems of attrition, we all agree that this is potentially a very serious problem.

In a country where workers move from subsistence farming to factory work, there are many serious difficulties. Indeed, some workers may find these difficulties to be insurmountable. This is not a question of change in physical location. The

Chapter 27   The Collaborative Model: Part II

worker might live just a few miles from the factory. Rather it is one of complete change in culture. The new factory worker undergoes total cultural shock, which we, living in the developed world, cannot even begin to comprehend.

In truth, regardless of management's skills and effort, the factory might well lose 50% of its workers in the course of the first six months. Dissatisfaction over income may be a factor, but when you take into account the combined cultural, sociological and psychological problems, wages are truly of secondary importance. Furthermore, while the loss of workers during the early days is not of great importance, losing workers after the sixth month is very serious. By then the factory has invested substantial time and effort in worker training. More to the point, the worker has made a real effort but has finally given up. To operate effectively, the factory must depend on the good reviews of its workforce. The well-run factory has no problems getting new workers because its existing workers recruit for them. COME TO WORK AT ABC. IT TAKES SOME GETTING USED TO, BUT AFTER A WHILE IT IS PRETTY GOOD. I HAVE MONEY IN MY POCKET. I AM MY OWN PERSON. MY SUPERVISOR TELLS ME THAT WITH A LITTLE MORE WORK, I CAN BE PROMOTED.

Then there is the matter of industrial action. In Brooklyn workers go on strike to achieve more: shorter hours, better conditions, higher wages or making Iron Man's birthday a public holiday. In Hawassa workers go on strike when they conclude that things will never improve. Here industrial action is truly an attack on the factory and specifically its management. It is a statement: WE HATE YOU. YOU SHOULD ALL DROP DEAD.

Relatively minor WORKER DISSATISFACTION has progressed to the ultimately large INDUSTRIAL ACTION. Just as there is a progression of outcomes, so too is there a progression of causes. What began as a $5 problem ultimately grows to a $50,000 problem and throughout the process, management has no idea what is going on in their midst, until Tuesday when zero workers show up at the factory.

Ours is very much a hands-on industry. In a successful operation, the boss knows just what is going on not only with his customers and his bankers but also on the factory floor. There are people with the experience necessary to avoid most of these problems who are able to take prompt action to solve any problems that occur to the satisfaction of all concerned.

Epic in Ethiopia

Epic Group is a transnational operation based in Hong Kong with factories in Bangladesh, Vietnam, Jordan and Hawassa. The owner, Ranjan Mahtani, is very much up to date with regard to systems and technology but at the same time very much old school with regard to his role in the operation. The Epic plan for Hawassa involves three factories of which the first, employing 2000 workers, is still very much a work in process. (The other two factories remain empty until the difficulties at the first factory have been ironed out).

The Guide to Cost-to-Value Analysis

Epic's solution to the potential problems has three parts:

Goals in the new global environment:
- Provide multiple country choices to our brands/customers;
- Provide duty-free options;
- Strike the right balance between efficiency and humanity in this highly competitive industry;
- Create sustainable business solutions.

Strategy for Hawassa:
- Employ a Crawl, Walk, Run business approach;
- Focus on culture and mind set;
- Focus on having the workforce be comfortable in the manufacturing environment;
- Focus on our people knowing the company and the end goals;
- Focus on providing better understanding to our people about supply chain;
- Build a strong foundation and then enlarge the footprints step-by-step in a sustainable manner.

Implementation for Hawassa:
- Three-week modular training capsule focused on skills and hygiene training;
- Monthly parents' days inviting workers' parents to see the facility to increase engagement;
- Develop skills among local employees to allow them to move up to management roles;
- Collaborate with government to explore further benefits to arrest potentially serious issues;
- Free meals, subsidized housing, transportation allowance, efficiency incentives and attendance bonus to increase employee well-being and earnings.

Ethiopia is set to grow to become a significant player in the global apparel trade. Epic will be part of that growth and journey, developing people and capacity to improve its operation, its people and the nation.

Ranjan and I are more than a generation apart but we do share much in common. We are both factory people. We are both hands-on. We both recognize that our people are our greatest asset and we are both self-taught.

I have to admit that this last attribute is not necessarily an asset. They say that experience is the best teacher. What they are not saying is that experience is also the most expensive teacher. We learn from our mistakes and all too often our mistakes are very costly.

Chapter 27 The Collaborative Model: Part II

There is much about the Stern Report that I disagree with. But there is one important area where there can be no disagreement: the problems raised in the report are real; they are serious; and the success of the entire Hawassa project may well rest on the ability to solve those problems.

Hawassa and our industry are in need of professional help. We do not need assistance on the garment production side. We are quite adept in that area. The problems at Hawassa shown in the report are not garment problems. They are of a different order and to solve these problems we need outside specialists: behavioral psychologists, sociologists, social economists, specialists in Ethiopian culture, and professionals with specific knowledge and experience in political risk analysis and negotiation.

Chapter 28
The Future of the Fashion Industry

This chapter was written by Emma Birnbaum.

The future of the fashion industry is more defined than the traditional players may think or wish to believe. It is now generally if begrudgingly accepted that the consumer is the major driver in retail sales. In fact the consumer is the *only* driver in sustainable industry growth. Any company that does not worship at the feet of the consumer does not stand a chance of surviving. Some retailers are at least trying but the rest of the supply chain – middlemen, factories, mills and farms – should be working towards serving the consumer and forgetting about the brand retailer.

This may seem counterproductive since, after all, the brand retailer is paying the bills. But today's blockbuster brands are overleveraged, lack innovation and are simply too big to change. If nothing else, the mass bankruptcies of the COVID crisis have revealed the fragility of the *modus operandi* of the previous industry. In order to remain relevant, the entire supply chain needs to focus on the consumer. Fortunately virtually all consumers have Instagram accounts so you can actually follow what they think, do and want in real time. Smart businesses are doing just that.

Subscription-based Retailers

Beauty Pie entered the cosmetics industry in 2015 and offers luxury cosmetics at factory prices to subscription members. The products range from lipstick and eye cream to perfume and shampoo, all selling at a fraction of regular retail prices. A member pays between £5 and £20 a month for a minimum period of three months. Each month the subscription can be redeemed for product with any leftover funds rolled to the next month. Beauty Pie manages to lower costs without sacrificing quality by cutting out the middleman, brick & mortar overhead, retailer markup, and expensive advertising. Here is the costing comparison for their Deluxe Moisture Body Crème.

The Guide to Cost-to-Value Analysis

	Deluxe Moisture Body Crème[1]			
	Traditional Retailer		Beauty Pie	
	Product	£15.44	Product	£15.44
	Safety		Safety	
	Testing & COS		Testing & COS	
	Fulfilment		Fulfilment	
	VAT		VAT	
	Middleman	£34.56	Middleman	n/a
	Shop Fits		Shop Fits	
	Retailer Mark-up		Retailer Mark-up	
	Celebrity Marketing		Celebrity Marketing	
	Total	**£50.00**	**Total**	**£14.44**

Beauty product consumers inevitably run out of multiple products at any given time and make ideal return customers. Subscription-based business models are also beginning to appear in the apparel industry. Savage X Fenty, founded in 2017 by none other than pop singer Rihanna, is a lingerie brand sold only online. It retails at an accessible price point, offers inclusive sizes, many colorways and edgy styles that appeal to a wide range of aesthetic tastes.

VIP Membership costs £50 per month, redeemable as credit upon purchase. A member is not committed to a monthly purchase and can avoid the £50 charge by logging into her account and clicking on "Skip the Month". The membership subscription can be cancelled at any time.

Both Beauty Pie and Savage X Fenty allow non-members to shop but they have to pay a significantly higher rrp (recommended retail price). For example, Beauty Pie's Super Healthy Skin defense serum costs £80 for non-members and only £12.07 for members. Savage X Fenty's Iridescent Lace Demi-Bra has a "Reg" price for non-members of £64 and a "VIP" price for members of £17.15.

Savage X Fenty has been accused of making their subscription model intentionally confusing. Customers think they are getting a great price but do not realize that they are enrolling in the monthly subscription program whose fees are only redeemable through further purchases although the unspent amount can be rolled over into the following month. Beauty Pie is far more transparent in their practices and has not received the same complaints.

---

1   *Beauty Pie Cost Transparency: https://www.beautypie.com/about-us*

Chapter 28   The Future of the Fashion Industry

On Savage X Fenty, models of all body types, sizes and skin tones are represented and consumers are encouraged to upload photos of themselves wearing and styling the items. This allows consumers to see how a style has been modified in order to meet each consumer's body type. The graphics below show the same bra on two women of very different sizes. The general design of the bra is the same – unlined, underwire, lace, demi-cut. However, the style has been adjusted to meet the needs of both smaller and larger frames. Figure 1 has a keyhole detail at the front, interior side boning, mesh-lined cups and nylon-based material composition. Figure 2 has sheer lace cups and a polyamide-based material composition.

Floral Lace Unlined Bra with X Charm

Model 5'8" wearing size 42E

The Guide to Cost-to-Value Analysis

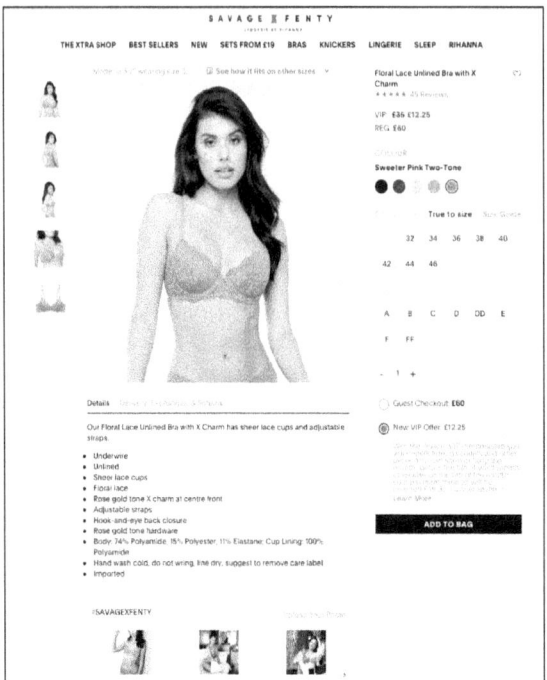

Model 5'7" wearing size 32B

The photos show consumers exactly how a style is modified to fit different consumers. It also demonstrates that the brand considers all its customers to be equally important, not just those filling a certain body type.

Victoria Secret's foundation for success – concentrating on consumers with model-type bodies – ultimately signalled its death knoll in today's more inclusive marketplace. Women now buy their own underwear to please themselves, not necessarily for their male partners. Savage X Fenty is a lingerie brand built by a woman for the culture of women – fun, fashionable, safe, inclusive, sexy, silly. There are plenty of fast fashion brands who can duplicate their formula to build up a network of repeat customers attracted by lower prices.

Insta-Brands

Instagram is probably the most innovative and disruptive game changer since the creation of the internet. Most e-commerce is limited to virtual catalogues, offering flat images of items clipped on models with little interaction and information. The style is photographed, Photoshopped, and copied and pasted next to a nondescript blurb. Instagram instead offers a unique space where brand retailers and consumers interact on the same platform, posting and tagging each other's images. Instagram allows consumers to view others personalizing, styling and wearing covetable items in a variety of real world settings. Those with the best photos, the most interesting styling and well curated feeds become very popular.

Chapter 28 The Future of the Fashion Industry

Over the past half-decade, some have such substantial and loyal followings that they have launched their own brands. These Instagrammers come from all over the globe. Some of the most well known are LPA, Orseund Iris, Cult Gaia (USA); I.AM.GIA, Poppy Lissiman (Australia); Réalisation (USA/Australia); Toteme (Sweden) and Rouje (France).

For the most part these brands were founded and run by women who began as consumers with blogs and a growing voice as influencers in the fashion industry. These budding designers and retailers carefully collate their insights into serving a defined consumer demographic who share their own tastes and lifestyles. Each brand has released it-items which are worn and promoted on social media by global style icons who are for the most part unpaid. The modest runs of stock almost invariably sell out. Of course, some brands don't make it. Competition is tough especially considering the brands are developing the infrastructure of their branch of the industry at the same time. Also it is difficult to find manufacturers willing to produce small runs of many styles which they require for their selling strategy.

The Consumer as the Retailer

As an industry, we need to begin reacting to consumer demands in real time. Consumers are educated; they know what they want and what constitutes "value" as defined in their eyes. In addition, they are wise to the business practices of extraneous costs and markups at the expense of the shopper. This is not to say that consumers are unwilling to pay for value. However, the value must be based on consumer demand and not on supply chain incompetence due to long lead times, excessive and unquantified overhead, and the inevitable markdowns.

In the airline and hotel industries prices fluctuate based on demand. But price fluctuation in fashion only goes one way – down. The inevitable 35% markdown might not seem so bad if the retailer was also marking up highly covetable products. In fact, this is already happening but traditional retailers aren't benefitting yet.

Savvy consumer-cum-sellers purchase and hoard desirable stock forcing consumers to flock to sites like eBay or Poshmart to purchase these designs. A typical example is the dress below designed for a special H&M collection which retailed at H&M for £35. At the exact same time, the dress was being sold on eBay for £83. The same seller sold a swimsuit on eBay for £32 and got a rave review from the buyer even though H&M was retailing the same swimsuit at only £24.

The Guide to Cost-to-Value Analysis

Screenshot of H&M UK Website

Screenshot of ebay.co.uk

In light of this new form of competition, what can traditional retailers do? H&M should certainly not unilaterally jack up their prices. But for global retailers like H&M, understanding the nuances of their consumer demographics is crucial. They need to study not just *what* sells better *where* but how much local consumers are willing to spend in each of their markets. After all, Bangkok Thailand and Manhattan New York may have similar demographics regarding aesthetic taste but very different income levels and environmental climates. Currently although there are slight differences in prices for each region, this is more based on what it costs to get the garment into the store and less on local consumer demand and purchasing power.

There are other online business practices that the fashion industry could consider. Travel sites such as Agoda and Booking.com reward frequent travellers with slashed prices, holiday packages and free upgrades. Airbnb provides statistically more reliable, frequent travellers greater and more direct access to listings. Sephora has an unlimited samples policy and insider benefits that include rewards, seasonal savings, free standard shipping, early

Chapter 28 The Future of the Fashion Industry

access to products and exclusive events. Unlike the apparel industry, loyalty is not limited to early access to sales (which, let's face it, are for products that no one wants anyway) but instead are genuine rewards for being consistent and loyal customers.

H&M offers a points system and 5% off vouchers for anyone bringing used clothing to the store. While this move is in the correct direction, H&M is still far behind the trends introduced by other far more data-driven industries. Furthermore, to date, H&M appears to be the only major player in the fashion industry attempting to integrate new retail trends.

Preloved Retail

Secondhand, used, vintage, preloved is a market dominated by consumer-driven retail. Gone are the days of trolling though musty, crusty Goodwill and Salvation Army racks. Today, secondhand shopping is as intuitive as a dating app, with a plethora of items that are photographed, tagged, and described online. Sellers are more than happy to negotiate and provide additional information and feedback.

In 2019 ThredUp and GlobalData published a report[2] comparing the growth of the U.S. used fashion market with the growth of the U.S. fast fashion market. They valued the preloved market in 2018 at $28 billion and the fast fashion market at $35 billion. Furthermore, ThredUp predicted that by 2028 preloved would reach $64 billion against fast fashion at $44 billion.

Depop, eBay, Etsy, ThredUp, Vinted, Rebelle, Vestiaire Collective are companies specializing in consumer-driven apparel resale. Sellers create a "boutique-style" personal page housing their listings with prices based on their determined value. Consumers are able to interact with sellers, negotiate price, and in some cases, trade items. In fact, sellers and consumers are the same people, frequently relisting items previously purchased on the app/website.

A typical item recently followed online showed a pair of boots which originally retailed for £275.00. The original purchaser never wore the boots and listed the unworn boots on Depop for £120.00. The purchaser negotiated the price to £100.00. Upon determining that thigh-high boots were not their style after a single wear, the second purchaser relisted and sold the boots for £100.00.

---

2   ThredUp 2019 Resale Report: https://www.thredup.com/resale/2019?tswc_redir=true

The Guide to Cost-to-Value Analysis

| 2
& Other Stories
Leather Thigh-High Boots
RRP £275.00 | **Depop**
Condition: Unworn
Price: £100.00 | **Depop**
Condition: Worn Once
Price: £100.00 |

This case clearly illustrates several characteristics of the reseller market. Some consumers will pay a premium for on-trend instant gratification and the ability to choose whatever item they want to buy. In this case the premium was £175.00, almost double the preloved price. As the preloved market mainstreams and more consumers flog their unworn or lightly worn goods, consumers will be less willing to pay a premium for choice simply because the offerings on the preloved market will more closely mirror those available on the brand retail market. Once high-street branded goods enter the preloved market, their price significantly drops and then levels off. The "unworn" boots and the "worn once" boot retailed for the same price of £100.00.

There is a category of resale items that retain or even increases in price. These generally occur with small, fashion-forward brands specializing in reasonably priced, high quality products with unusual designs appealing to a specific consumer demographic defined by age, aesthetic taste, social media interaction, and economic class. In the evening dress by Rat & Boa shown on next page, the price differential between new from the brand and worn once on Depop is only £35. First choice, while still valuable, is not as valuable as the pleasure of owning and wearing the Rat & Boa dress. This indicates that quality and great design are highly prized, and that light wear and tear is not detrimental to perceived value.

Chapter 28   The Future of the Fashion Industry

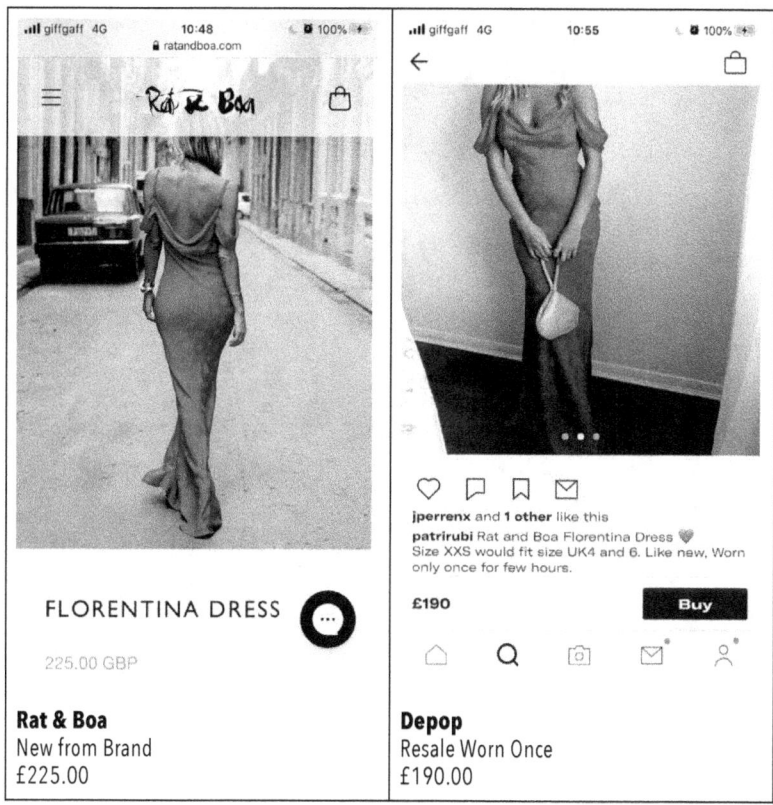

In general, for savvy consumers, the preloved market means that the buyer can own a constantly changing, on-trend wardrobe akin to the offering of fast fashion without losing any money. In fact, the consumer's ability to resell their previously worn items for the same or similar price implies a future where consumers will spend more on a single item safe in the knowledge that the money can be redeemed later down the line.

So far the major players of the traditional fashion industry have almost no stake in the preloved market. They also have no answer to resellers who are able to achieve greater profits from buying up and selling their own highly prized items. The point of all these trends is that the consumer has already become the center of the fashion industry. Markets that the so-called professionals consider as secondary or irrelevant are in fact highly active and growing at a far greater speed than anyone – even those who think they are running the show – realizes.

Chapter 29
Towards the Industry Yet to Come

This chapter was written by David Birnbaum.

This is a book about change. Its message is simple: **CHANGE OR DIE**.

I am a third-generation garmento. My grandmother was in the business as was her son, my father. Same industry, but my grandmother would never have been able to comprehend what my father did much less how he did it. My father was a very knowledgeable man, indeed a person ahead of his time. But my father would not have lasted five minutes in today's industry.

Change is never easy, even for those of us for whom change is a vocation. Professionals call me the garment guru , the one on the cutting edge of change. However, to maintain the respect of my peers, I too must change. For this reason this book has been the first collaboration with my daughter Emma whose knowledge and insight of the new industry will keep us on the cutting edge.

The book is about change from the past to the present and from the present to the future. We can see change through the different perspectives of industry models, operational methodology and the definition of the key players.

Industry Models

1. The competitive model dating back to the beginning of the modern global garment industry in the aftermath of WWII when customers cared only about FOB price and looked at their suppliers as disposable tools. Factories looked at their workers in the same way, as disposable tools to be thrown away when not needed.
2. The cooperative model, the way most successful companies operate today, where customers and their suppliers work together to reduce costs to benefit both sides.
3. The collaborative model, the way of the future, when customer and supplier enter into a virtual partnership that allows for operations previously thought impossible.

Methodology

1. The traditional way when factories were simply product makers.
2. The current way when factories move from product maker to service provider.

Redefining the Players

1. The traditional way when factories were limited to production; middlemen limited to passive follow up; and the customer was king.
2. The current way with the introduction of the consumer as a dominant player.

The Guide to Cost-to-Value Analysis

3. The current way when factories have also become customers as they increasingly develop their own in-house brands and retail operations, the middleman moving towards proactive support for both the customer and the supplier, and the customer being dethroned by the consumer, the new king.

I have been around for a very long time and I have seen a lot. I have seen remarkable change and the success that change has brought to those who embraced that change. I have also seen the failure of those who remained stuck in the dead past.

The Customer Side

Towards the end of the 20th century, we have seen plenty of what I consider to be omnivore events where retailers who had been successful operators for over a century were literally eaten up by other more dynamic retailers. Now as the world grapples with COVID-19, we are seeing a second omnivore wave where the survivors of the earlier extinction are themselves falling prey to new and more dynamic retailers.

At this very moment, as retail managers plan for the post-COVID-19 industry, some still hold to the belief that nothing will have changed.

Yes, they argue, WE ARE GOING THROUGH DIFFICULT TIMES. THE VIRUS ENDEMIC AND THE RECESSION HAVE CAUSED SERIOUS UPSET. HOWEVER, ONCE THIS SHORT-TERM DISRUPTION ENDS, THINGS WILL RETURN TO NORMAL.

Their strategy is to win by doing nothing. THE CURRENT CRISIS WILL PUSH THE SMALL PLAYERS TO BANKRUPTCY LEAVING US IN AN EVEN STRONGER POSITION.

With regards to a consumer-dominated society, their strategy is yet again to do nothing. WE, THE MAJOR RETAILERS AND BRANDS, HAVE ONLY TO NOD OUR HEADS AND PAY LIP SERVICE, BUT NEVER FORGET THAT CONSUMERS ARE STUPID. THEY DO NOT KNOW WHAT THEY WANT UNTIL WE — THE EDUCATED AND THE KNOWLEDGEABLE — TELL THEM WHAT THEY WANT.

Yet in this new real world, survival depends on first determining what the consumer wants and secondly, giving it to them.

To understand just what the consumer wants, we must first recognize that design does not take place in a vacuum. Design does not begin with talented men and women sitting down with a blank sheet of paper and in a sudden burst of inspiration drawing the perfect, most saleable garment. The design is rather the final step in a process. No person, regardless of talent and/or craft actually invented fast fashion or athleisure. Those are both physical manifestations of the changes going through the world today.

From the outset fashion has always followed social change. From the complex

Chapter 29   Towards the Industry Yet to Come

and suffocating fashion of the late 18th century to the simpler more comfortable empire design of the early 19th, through the era of corsets and whalebone to the freedom of the 1920s flappers, the staid look of the 1930s, and on and on, fashion and social change has always gone hand in hand.

To succeed in today's marketplace we must first understand the consumer:

- We are going through a difficult period;
- People are filled with fear, anger and resentment towards the establishment;
- People believe that an oligarchy of the rich and powerful are exploiting everyone;
- Society is open to revolution.

For the customer side, this is a period of CHANGE OR DIE. Sadly, many established retailers have decided dying is preferable to change.

The Supplier Side

Over the past decades as the industry has changed, the supplier side has gradually moved from simple product makers to more complex service suppliers. Factories now fall into three categories. At the top are the full-service suppliers with the facilities to provide cutting-edge services. These include the billion-dollar transnational factory groups, which because of their size and importance, are able to invest in centralized specialty departments including engineering, advanced IT, with the latest management techniques staffed by leading specialists in their respective fields.

These full-service suppliers also include the strategic suppliers who, because of their very special facilities, are able to charge premium prices and are therefore able to invest in specialists necessary to develop and implement these important services. Increasingly these full-service factories are reaching out directly to consumers to try to understand consumer needs and demands.

At the other extreme are zero-service factories. These are restricted to cutting and making only, offering no services. For the most part, their production is limited to basic commodity garments. These factories, and in many cases their entire national industries, are trapped at the bottom. Since their customers come to them only for basic commodities with no services, their customers do not look to them for services with the result that the factories do not see the need to develop services. Their view of the garment industry world is one where low FOB price is everything.

The largest group are the normal-service factories in the middle. They want to develop services but believe they are unable to do so. For well over 25 years, I have heard the same lament: OUR CUSTOMERS WANT SERVICES. WE WANT TO PROVIDE SERVICES. BUT THE CUSTOMERS DO NOT WANT TO PAY FOR THOSE SERVICES.

The Guide to Cost-to-Value Analysis

For a very long time, the three sectors operated in a state of equilibrium where everyone could make money, and everyone could survive. That equilibrium has now been broken.

The advent of the consumer – the third and dominant player – is about to change everything. In this new industry, the factory that fails to meet the needs of the consumer will not survive because their customer will not survive.

The full-service factories will enjoy the greatest benefit because they will be at the cutting edge of service, having prepared for this new industry long before there was a new industry to prepare for.

The zero-service factories for the most part will go the way of the dinosaurs because like the dinosaurs they will be unable to adapt to the new environment of a smaller, more agile industry based on smaller orders and faster lead times. Giant zero-service factories with 2400 machines divided into 30 lines, each with 80 machines, built to produce 2-3 orders per month, each averaging 500,000 plus units will be unable to restructure into 75 lines, each with 30 machines, built to produce 30-50 orders each averaging 25,000 units.

It is the middle category, the normal-service factories, that will face the greatest challenge. To survive in this new industry, they will have to develop the services necessary to meet the consumers' needs. Doing nothing and waiting for their customers to pay for services will no longer be an option. To survive, normal-service factories must move forward. To move forward they must find a way to develop the required services while at the same time finding a customer who will pay for those services. There are a wide range of strategies. Each factory must find one.

The Consumer Side

The consumer is currently in a very special position. While retail and brand managers have yet to recognize that in this changing industry they have lost control, consumers have yet to recognize – in this same changing industry – the full extent of their control. At the same time, while factories must develop strategies to meet consumers' demands, consumers must recognize that many of their most important demands can be met only by the factory. In this regard, the consumer and the factory must work together for mutual benefit.

Consumer demands in this new industry fall into two distinct areas:

- Going forward, consumers will want many of the same things that consumers have always wanted: interesting design, good fit, good make and low price.
- Consumers will also have other demands. While in a segmented market, different consumers will still want different things, there is a growing consensus of what they do *not* want. What they *do* want is determined by social change.

Chapter 29 Towards the Industry Yet to Come

In this regard to understand what is happening we need only return to the beginning of this chapter. We have simply to look at the society in which we live.

- We are going through a difficult period.
- People are filled with fear, anger and resentment towards the establishment.
- People believe that an oligarchy of the rich and powerful are exploiting everyone.
- Society is open to revolution.

Consumers do not want unsustainability and pollution. They do not want the clothing on their backs, sewn in sweat shops where ten-year-old children or women are forced to work 70-hour weeks with only one day off per month, unsafe conditions, earning wages below subsistence.

Enter the **INFLUENCERS** – the superstars of the internet – young men and women each with millions of followers, advising those followers what to buy. It is only a matter of time before these influencers move from design, fit, make and price to sweatshops, child labor, excessive overtime, unsafe working conditions and slave wages. The first minute a single major influencer makes the shift to ethical behavior it will already be too late for retailers, brands, factories and national garment exporting industries. They will already be out of business.

Glossary

3D Pattern Making	Because the human body is a three-dimensional object while a garment pattern is two-dimensional, traditional patternmaking is never accurate. Sophisticated 3D computer modeling seeks to overcome this difficulty.
Agent	Independent company that oversees production on behalf of import customers and is paid on a commission basis, typically between 5%-15%
Analogue	Device or system that represents changing values as continuously variable physical quantities. A traditional clock with hour and minute hands is an analogue as opposed to a digital clock that shows the time in hours, minute and seconds.
Ancillary Services	Design assists such as producing color standards, spec sheets, tech sheets, style reviews, lab dip and/or strikeoff approvals to send to factories
Artificial Intelligence	IT term for computer program which is able to "learn" from experience
Basic Cost Sheet	List of garment costs usually limited to factors traditionally thought to be areas involving the factory: fabric, trim and CM (labor, overhead, profit)
Brand Importer	A company that designs and arranges for overseas production for its own account. The styles are wholesaled to retailers under the importer's own label. Typically markups are on the order of 55%.
Branding	Process where an object, a process, or an operation is redefined and shown to the public as something of value
Brick and Mortar	Traditional retail store with a physical location as opposed to an e-commerce retailer where the sales location is virtual
Buyers' Market	Situation where the customer is the dominant force determining the success or failure of a product, a company or an industry
Buying	Process whereby the customer purchases a completed product and the supplier provides all materials including fabric and trim (see Sourcing)
Buying Office	Wholly-owned subsidiary of an importer or retailer that carries out the same functions as an independent agent, to oversee production. Typically the importer/retailer allocates a percentage commission.
Capacity	Total number of units that a factory is capable of producing in a specified period of time
Collaborative Model	Third historical trend in relationship between the customer and the supplier, wherein they form a partnership that allows both sides, working together, to do something not previously possible

The Guide to Cost-to-Value Analysis

Competitive Model	First historical trend in relationship between the customer and the supplier wherein the relationship is totally confrontational and the customer cares only to negotiate the lowest FOB price. By definition a zero-sum game.
Compliance	Ethical standard defining a company's relationship with its workers, including wages, working hours, days off, worker safety and worker rights
Consumer	Final end customer of a product
Cooperative Model	Second historical trend in relationship between the customer and supplier wherein both sides work together to increase profit on both sides for the most part through product cost reduction
Coordination Department	Cross-discipline section within a factory responsible to provide real-time information of work in process for each order; communication between operational departments and related parties such as merchandising and logistics; notification on a timely basis to relevant parties of any delays
Cost	Amount the supplier pays for a specific product or service (see Price)
Costing	Sum total of all costs related a specific order. The costing exists even when the company does not know all cost factors, fails to list specific cost factors, or lists them incorrectly.
Cost Sheet	List of costs prepared by the company corresponding to their understanding of the costing
CSR	Corporate Social Responsibility, typically including compliance, pollution and sustainability
Customer Care Team	Cross-discipline section within a factory consisting of merchandiser, designers, patternmakers, QA, and QC where the team is dedicated to a single customer or small number of customers
Customer Side	Designation including importers, retailers and brands and one of the three groups, along with Supplier and Consumer, constituting those responsible for the traditional supply chain
Cut & Make (CM)	Making cost of garment including factory labor, overhead and profit
Cut Make & Trim (CMT)	Cost of the garment less the main fabric, including all submaterials and making costs
Delivery Duty Paid (DDP)	Price of product up to and including delivery to the customer's warehouse or distribution center including total garment cost, overseas freight, insurance, import tariff, customs clearance charges and inland freight
Design Integrity	Situation whereby the sample follows the designer's concept as reflected in the sample and where the stock coincides with the sample
Digital	Term in information theory describing a discrete and discontinuous representation of information or works

Glossary

Diocletian	Roman emperor from 244-311ce responsible for introducing the first textile quota
Discontinuity	Occurs when a step in the manufacturing process is carried out without sufficient information of the steps that have gone before. For example, a technical sketch is drawn from the designer's sketch without complete understanding of the actual design concept resulting in every subsequent step taking the style further away from the original design.
Disruptive Innovation	Occurs when a new concept or product is introduced that is so radically different that it displaces the pre-existing market
Distribution Center	Retail logistics term for a location where an order imported in bulk is broken down to be reshipped to individual branch stores
Duplicate	In the product development process, the first piece is the original "sample" while all further iterations are "duplicates". In practice, while the designer may go through several duplicates before finally approving the design, the last and accepted duplicate becomes the same as the sample.
Dynamic Cost Sheet	Where costs not traditionally listed on a cost sheet affect final listed costs. For example, for products made in countries with free-trade agreements (FTA), higher fabric costs while raising FOB price actually reduce final costs when local fabric is granted for duty-free access.
E-commerce	Sales channel where products are sold directly to consumers via internet as opposed to brick and mortar stores
Easter Bunny	Character which defines typical American's feelings about rabbits and important for understanding the angora sweater case study
Epic-in-Ethiopia Plan	Strategy created by Epic Group to allow for more efficient production in Hawassa (Ethiopia)
Extrinsic Cost	Important factor in the cooperative model whereby investments and efforts on one side provide reduced costs on the other. For example, product development carried out by the factory leads to reduced cost for the customer.
Fast Fashion	Term often misused to define styles provided quickly by stores to be the first with the latest item
Fast Turn	Manufacturing system allowing markedly reduced factory production lead times
Fit	Garment measurements that relate to body shape
Flying Shuttle	18th century innovation, one of the first in the Industrial Revolution, allowing for faster and higher quality weaving
FOB	Free on Board: Invisible line represented by the ship's railing defining the limits of supplier responsibility. When the goods cross the invisible line, responsibility for the goods shifts to the customer.

The Guide to Cost-to-Value Analysis

Full Value Cost	Total cost of the garment up to and including the markdown
Full Value Cost Sheet	List of costs of the garment up to and including the markdown
Gap	Occurs when a necessary step in the manufacturing process is not carried out at all. For example, samples are sent to the customer without a costing. Should the sample be accepted by the customer, radical design changes might then be required to fit the style into the customer's target price range.
Garment Buying	Early method of garment purchase by the customer from the supplier, whereby the supplier provides all components including fabric and trim
Garment Sourcing	Later method of garment purchase whereby the customer negotiates direct with the fabric and trims suppliers and having reached an agreed price passes the name of the designated suppliers and the prices to the supplier who pays for the materials
Garmento	Garment industry argot for an industry professional
GPS	Global Positioning System: satellite navigation system to determine the real-time ground location of any object, at sea or land
Greater China	China, Hong Kong and Macao
Hit Rate	Percentage of orders generated from styles designed by the factory
Horizontal Integration	Entire process required from preproduction, production, and postproduction of a specific product, from first designer sketch to stock garment arrival at the customer's designated location
HTS	Harmonized Tariff Schedule: universal system to define products for import tariff purposes, e.g. section 61 for knit garments; section 62 for woven garments
ILO	International Labor Organization: United Nations organization set up to cover all areas involving workers with 40 branches globally
Import Office	Division of a retail company where in-house private label processes are carried out. This includes design, sourcing, logistics, etc.
Influencer	An individual, typically originally a consumer and not an industry professional, with a sizable following on social media who has established trust and is able to influence followers to make purchasing decisions
Innovation	New idea, method or product
Insta-brand	Brands which are launched, promoted and sold directly to consumers on the social media platform Instagram
Instagram	Online photo-sharing application and social network platform that is a favored venue for influencers

Glossary

Intrinsic Cost	Important factor in the cooperative model whereby investments and efforts for either supplier or customer provides reduced cost benefits for the same side. For example, increased productivity provides greater profits for the supplier.
Job Costing	List of total costs for a specific order calculated after shipment to ensure accuracy
Joint-cost problem	Series of costs for a number of related products all developed simultaneously and which therefore cannot be broken down separately
Lab Dip	Fabric swatch submitted by the supplier for piece-dyed color approval
Landed Duty Paid (LDP)	Price of the product up to and including customs clearance including total garment cost, overseas freight, insurance, import tariff and customs clearance charges
LDP	Landed Duty Paid: includes FOB + freight + import duty
Lean Manufacturing	Manufacturing methodology to reduce waste and lead times by use of multi-tasked teams rather than traditional assembly lines and characterized by zero work in process at end of each working day
Loading	Percentage added to each garment unit to cover a specific cost. Examples include: 5% buying office and 20% retailer's import office commissions, wholesalers' mandatory contributions for retailer advertising, etc.
Low Season	Period in a seasonal industry with reduced demand
Mass Customization	Ability to rapidly produce large quantities in many sizes through computerized systems with little or no increased costs
MBA	Master of Business Administration: graduate university degree for business professionals
Merchandise Manager (Retailer)	Person responsible to ensure that the each department meets its goals with regard to volume and profit. Usually the buyer's boss.
Merchandiser (Factory)	Person responsible for all communications between the customer and the factory
Merchandiser (Importer)	Person responsible to ensure that the style designs meet the needs of the target customer. Usually the designer's boss.
Modelista	Traditionally part of a two-person design team, where the designer (stylista) creates the design concept and the modelista develops that concept into the sample garment
Money-in-the-pocket Principle	Methodology common during early years of the global garment industry where the factory supplier adds an amount to every cost item to allow for forced reductions during subsequent negotiations with the buyer
Monopsomy	Market in which there is only one buyer
Multi-tasked	Refers to special skill-set factory sewer capable of multiple operations which allows for production of smaller, higher quality orders

The Guide to Cost-to-Value Analysis

Negative Value	Value analysis cost term where a particular service does not reduce costs relative to value but which is nevertheless necessary. For example, sustainability has negative value; while it does not add value because the consumer will not pay more for a sustainable product, the consumer may not buy a product which lacks sustainability.
Net Profit	Profit that remains after allowing for all costs including overhead
Net Retail Price	Price after allowing for markdowns
No-bottom-price Principle	Methodology common in the early years of the global garment industry where the customer would not accept any price regardless of amount until confident that factory would not make further price reductions
On-Demand Cutting	System of garment cutting which allows for cutting against the order, even when the order is only one piece
Open Data	Methodology where the supplier provides the customer with an accurate detailed cost sheet, including net profit, and will not further negotiate. Open data is limited to strategic suppliers and allows the customer to estimate the FOB price during product development.
Open Sourcing	Methodology where the customer is able to calculate all cost factors, thus reducing variables solely to number of minutes per unit. As a result, the customer negotiates cost-per-minute for all orders placed in a set period of time.
Overhead	All ongoing business expenses unrelated to materials and direct labor and therefore non-variable
Parallax Gap	Astronomical term for the apparent change in position of an object in fact caused by the change in position of the viewer
Pick & Pack	Important operation in e-commerce logistics where a bulk shipment is broken down and repackaged for individual customers.
Preloved Retail	Retail model dealing with secondhand goods; preloved retail is generally consumer-to-consumer as opposed to business-to-consumer
Price	Amount the customer pays for a specific product or service (see Cost)
Private Label Importer	Company which designs and arranges for overseas production on behalf of retailers. Each style is imported exclusively for a specific retail customer and sold under the retailer's label. Typical wholesale mark-up is in the range of 30%.
Product Development	Process from first designer sketch to final sample approval
Productivity	Number of units produced within a specific length of time with the same number of workers
Products from Hell	Most difficult items to produce, including bridalwear, fashion bras and girls size 6-12 dresses

Glossary

Pure Play	Business model focused on a single product, activity, service or retail channel
Quality Assurance (QA)	Process which takes place before garment making commences to ensure that the style can be produced by the factory correctly, efficiently and at a reasonable cost
Quality Control (QC)	Process which takes place during the garment-making process to ensure that the materials are correct and that the garment is produced to the correct quality standard and quality level
Quality Level	Along with Quality Standard, one of two quality facets. Refers to the degree to which each operation in the garment-making process is carried out correctly. The higher the quality standard, the more difficult it is to maintain quality level.
Quality Standard	One of two facets of quality. Refers to the specified steps for each operation in the garment-making process. The higher the quality standard, the more difficult it is to maintain quality level.
Quick Response	Ability of the factory to provide re-orders with short lead times
Quota	Quantitative import (or export) limitation
Sell Through Rate	Degree to which a style is sold to end consumer at full retail price
Shape	Body measurements (see Fit)
Size	Alphanumeric term classifying range of fits (S-M-L, 4-14 etc.)
Skill Set	Term defining job specifications based on specific knowledge and abilities
SME	Small and Medium Enterprises. In the garment industry SME connotes small factories.
SME Center	Structure designed to provide assists for a national e-commerce factory sector
Soft Cost	In cost value analysis, soft cost factors are those which are difficult to quantify in monetary terms, e.g. quality, reliability, ethical behavior, etc.
Solidarity	International arm of the U.S. AFL-CIO labor union
Sourcing	Process whereby the customer negotiates the price for all materials (fabric and trim), then designates the suppliers leaving the factory to pay for the materials which it can then include in their FOB price
Space-Time Continuum	Einsteinian concept wherein neither space nor time are fixed in the universe but are interrelated factors. What is true of the universe is equally true of the garment industry where everything – cost, price, profit and success – are related to lead times.
Speed-to-market	Manufacturing system designed to reduce total lead time
Standard Garment Sourcing Model (SGSM)	Traditional paradigm for garment sourcing, first created sixty years ago

The Guide to Cost-to-Value Analysis

Static Cost Sheet	Traditional cost sheet typically includes FOB cost (material, trim, CM)
Strategic Supplier	Factory of great importance to customer
Strikeoff	Fabric swatch submitted by the supplier for print or yarn-dyed approval
Structural	Refers to organization of a company including machinery and employees (See Systemic)
Subcontractor	Factory employed by another primary factory to produce goods for the primary factory on behalf of a customer
Subscription-based Retailer	Retail model whereby customers are required to pay a recurring fee at regular intervals for access to products or services at reduced prices
Supplier Side	Typically includes factories (see Customer Side)
Supply Chain	List of steps in a process typically including product development, production and postproduction.
Sustainability	Production process that strives to avoid depletion of natural resources in order to maintain ecological balance
Sweatshop	Pejorative term for a factory with poor compliance
Systemic	Refers to method by which the company structure is utilized (see Structural)
Tariff	Tax placed on imports
Trading Company	Independent company performing a wide range of services on behalf of import customers including overseeing production whose fees come from commissions paid by the customer, by the factory, are included in the garment price, or a combination of some or all of the above.
Trial Orders	Part of speed-to-market, whereby the factory produces small quantities of a style to allow the customer to measure initial retail consumer reaction
Trim	Generic term referring to submaterials used in garment manufacture
Twitter	American microblogging and social networking service on which users post and interact with messages known as "tweets"
Universal Factory Supplier	Factory capable of supplying product both competitively and to the customers' needs from anywhere in the world
Vertical Integration	Entire process beginning at material production through garment making, i.e., from spinning to finished garment
Vintage Clothing	Used clothes, particularly fashion, available for resell
Work in Process	Refers to unfinished product undergoing manufacturing. Also accounting term for monetary value of unfinished order and broken down by process, i.e. cutting, sewing, pressing, packing
Work in Progress	Accounting term referring to number of unfinished units. Frequently also referred to as Work in Process.

Glossary

Zero-sum	Game theory term where the total amount won equals the total amount lost. FOB price negotiations between customer and factory is a zero-sum game.

Index

3D pattern making 137, 169
Agent .... iii, 8, 55, 58, 65-67, 93, 98-99, 129, 132-133, 138-140, 169
Agoda 158
Air freight 12
Airbnb 158
Amazon 77, 140
Analogue 79-81, 83, 169
Angora 38-39, 171
Artificial intelligence 85, 169
Basic cost sheet 3, 11-12, 27-28, 41, 46, 48, 53-54, 97, 169
Beauty Pie 153-154
BF Skinner 87
Booking.com 158
Branch factory 8
Branding 101, 103, 105, 169
Bras 44, 174
Brick and Mortar (B&M) 107
Bridalwear 44, 174
Bundling 5
Buying office 49, 51, 115, 131-133, 146, 169, 173
CAFTA-DR 63
Cambodia .... xiv, 18, 63, 103
Capacity 5, 7, 13, 16, 21-25, 48, 111, 150, 169
Caribbean countries xiv
Child labor 38, 75, 167
China .... iii, 11, 16, 18-19, 34, 47-48, 50, 122-123, 143, 145-146, 172
CM .... xii-xiii, 3-4, 7, 11-12, 14-15, 17, 27-31, 44-46, 49-50, 53-55,
              58-59, 63-68, 93, 114, 137, 148, 169-170, 176
Collaborative Model .... xv, 73, 75, 77, 82, 101, 109, 121, 123, 127, 140,
              143, 145-147, 149, 151, 163, 169
Competitive Model .. xiv-xv, 42, 63, 65-66, 68-69, 73, 97, 125, 163, 170
Compliance 37-38, 60, 75, 102, 113, 142, 145, 148, 170, 176
Cooperative Model .... xiv-xv, 27, 67, 69, 73, 127, 163, 170-171, 173
Coordination department 24-25
Cost .... i, ix-x, xii-xiii, xv, 3-8, 11-25, 27-32, 34, 37-38, 40-55,
     57-60, 63-69, 73-74, 76, 80, 82, 86, 88-95, 97-100, 102, 104, 108-114,
         116, 118-122, 125-127, 129-130, 132-134, 137-140, 142, 146-148,
              150, 153-154, 156-158, 160, 163-164, 166, 169-176
Cost sheet 3-4, 6, 8, 11-12, 14, 27-28, 41-42, 46-55, 57-58, 66, 68,
              93-95, 97, 99-100, 113, 125, 169-172, 174, 176
Costing .... ix, xii-xiii, xv, 4-9, 22, 42, 57-58, 67, 97-100, 139, 153, 170,
              172-173
COVID-19 164
Crompton's spinning mule 85
CSR 37-38, 40, 60-61, 102, 137, 146, 170
Customer .... ix-xv, 3-5, 8-9, 11-13, 19, 22, 24-25, 27,
     29-31, 34-35, 37-39, 41-54, 57-60, 63-69, 73-75, 77, 82, 87-91, 94-95,

179

Index

    97-103, 105, 107-110, 113-114, 116-120, 123, 125-127, 129, 131-134, 137, 139-141, 145-146, 149-150, 154, 156, 159, 163-166, 169-177

Customer Care Team 119-120, 170
Customer side .... xi-xii, 13, 37, 42, 58, 77, 97, 125, 127, 164-165, 170, 176
Cutting .... v, xiv, 4-5, 7, 14, 16, 45, 82-83, 91, 108, 111, 139, 142, 153, 163, 165-166, 174, 176
DDP 55, 58-59, 65-66, 68, 93-94, 98-99, 137-140, 170
Depop 159-161
Design integrity 20, 30, 69, 116, 170
Digital 79-81, 83, 91, 169-170
Diocletian 143, 171
Disruptive Innovation 91, 121, 137, 171
Distribution Center 55, 58, 66, 68, 93, 98-99, 170-171
Dominican Republic 129, 134
Duplicate 28-30, 156, 171
Dyeing 24-25
Dynamic cost sheet 171
E-commerce .... xv, 76-77, 82, 107-111, 113-114, 137, 139-140, 156, 169, 171, 174-175
Easter bunny 39, 171
eBay 157-159
Elon Musk 121
Epic Group 149, 171
Ethiopia 31-33, 35, 147-150, 171
Etsy 140, 159
Extrinsic cost 13, 27-29, 171
Fabric .... ix, xiii, 4-5, 7, 11-12, 21, 25, 27, 30-32, 44, 46-47, 51, 53, 57-58, 63-64, 66, 79-81, 86, 91, 110-111, 113-114, 116, 122, 143, 169-173, 175-176
Fast fashion 156, 159, 161, 164, 171
Fast turn .... xiv, 8, 57-58, 89, 171
Finishing 24-25
Fit 38, 74, 79-81, 83, 85, 107, 115, 154, 166-167, 171-172, 175
Flying Shuttle 85, 171
FOB .... ix, xii-xiv, 3, 5, 7, 11, 15, 17, 19-20, 27-30, 46, 51, 53-55, 57-60, 63-68, 73, 93-95, 97-100, 114, 120, 125, 137-140, 163, 165, 170-171, 173-177
Freight 12, 55, 58, 65-67, 93, 98-99, 114, 138-140, 170, 173
Full value cost sheet 53-55, 99-100, 172
Gap 50-52, 60, 81, 138, 140-141, 143, 172, 174
Garment buying 12, 47, 53, 63, 172
Garment sourcing .... ix, xiii, 12, 47, 53, 63, 172, 175
Garmento .... ix-x, 126, 141-143, 163, 172
General Motors 101
Germany 19, 47, 80
Goodwill 159

Index

GPS 79, 172
H&M 81, 157-159
Hawassa Industrial Park 147
Hong Kong .... iii, ix, 18, 109, 126, 145, 149, 172
Horizontal Integration 137-138, 172
HTS 19, 33, 172
I.AM.GIA 157
In-store 54-55, 58-59, 66, 68, 81, 93-94, 98-99
India .... iii, xi, 18, 47, 82, 103
Inditex 85-86, 126
Influencer 102-105, 157, 167, 172
Informed cynicism 75, 105
Innovation 89, 91, 93, 121-123, 127, 137, 153, 171-172
Insta-Brands 156
Instagram 107, 153, 156, 172
Intrinsic cost 13, 15, 17-19, 28, 137, 173
IT .... iii-iv, ix-xv, 3, 5-9, 11-12, 15-18, 20, 22, 24-25, 27-28, 30, 32, 34-35, 37-45, 47-51, 53-54, 57, 59-61, 63-65, 67, 69, 73-77, 79-81, 83, 85-89, 94-95, 97-98, 100-105, 107-110, 113-118, 120-123, 125-126, 129, 132-134, 137-143, 145-151, 153-154, 156-161, 163-167, 169, 171, 174-175
Italy .... xi, 19, 47, 80
Japan 34, 122
Jeans 44, 82-83
Jeff Bezos 39
Job costing 4, 6-9, 98, 173
Joint-cost problem 5, 173
Kmart 122
Knitting 24-25
Labor union 104-105, 175
LDP 11, 68, 173
Lean manufacturing 86, 173
Lenzi 74
Levi Strauss 103
Low season 6, 9, 43, 45, 173
LPA 157
Marks & Spencer 81, 103
Masaccio 74
Mass customization 82, 173
Matthias Knappe xi
MBA .... xiii, 3, 50, 173
Mickey Drexler 50
Modelista 118, 173
Money-in-the-pocket principle ix
Morris Birnbaum .... ix-x
Multi-tasked 87, 91, 111-112, 121, 173
Myanmar 31, 33-35, 146

181

Index

Negative value 37, 39, 174
Net profit 3-4, 6-8, 17, 45, 53, 58-59, 68-69, 94, 98, 100, 114, 116,
120, 174
Net retail 51, 55, 58, 66, 68, 93, 95, 98-99, 137-140, 174
No-bottom-price principle ix
On-demand cutting 174
Open data 77, 174
Open Sourcing 12, 63-67, 69, 174
Original design .... xv, 113, 115, 118, 171
Orseund Iris 157
Oscar de la Renta 87
Overhead ..... xiii, 3-7, 9, 12, 14-17, 23, 27-30, 45-46, 53, 55, 58, 63, 65-
67, 93, 114, 146, 153, 157, 169-170, 174
Packing 5, 14, 49, 176
Parallax gap 141, 143, 174
Philip Van Heusen 146
Pick & Pack 16, 31, 112-114, 174
Pollution .... xi, 145, 167, 170
Poppy Lissiman 157
Porsche 41
Poshmart 157
Preloved Retail 159, 174
Pressing 5, 14, 176
Price .... ix-x, xii-xiv,
3, 5, 9, 11-12, 19-20, 28-29, 31, 37-39, 41, 43, 45-47, 49-55, 57, 59-60,
63-68, 73-75, 82, 94-95, 97-98, 102, 107, 110, 113, 115-116, 120, 123,
125, 129, 137-140, 153-154, 156-161, 163, 165-167, 170-177
Primark 81
Product development .... xiv, 8, 13, 27, 53-55,
57-59, 66-69, 85-86, 89, 91, 93-94, 98-99, 118-119, 123, 125-126, 129,
132, 137, 139-140, 171, 174, 176
Productivity .... ix, 13, 16-17, 46-47, 53, 63-64, 85-87, 113, 137, 173-174
Products from hell 44-45, 174
PVH 146-148
Quality 30, 38, 41-45, 49-52, 60, 63, 69, 75, 82, 85, 87, 97, 100, 121,
142, 153, 160, 171, 173, 175
Quick response 58, 89, 99, 129, 175
Quota 109, 143, 171, 175
Rana Plaza 145-146
Rat & Boa 160-161
Réalisation 157
Rebelle 159
Reseller 160-161
Rihanna 154
Salvation Army 159
Sample making 27-31, 46, 49, 118-119
Santa Maria Novella 74

Index

Savage X Fenty 154-156
Schedule 21-25, 88, 172
Schmata 63, 126
Seasonality 5-6, 42-43
Sephora 158
Shape 75, 79-81, 85, 115, 171, 175
Sir Simon Marks 50
Size .... .21, 23, 28, 44-46, 57-58, 60, 79-83, 91, 94, 107-109, 121, 154-156, 165, 173-175
Skill set 120, 175
SME 76, 101, 109-114, 175
SME Center 110-114, 175
Soft cost 60, 175
Soft technology 85-87
Solidarity 104, 175
Sourcing .... iii, ix, xiii, 12, 27, 37, 47, 53, 60, 63-67, 69, 99-100, 110, 125-127, 137-138, 146, 169, 172, 174-175
South Asia xiv
Southeast Asia 15, 146
Space-time continuum 129, 131, 133, 175
Spain .... xi, 19, 47
Speed-to-market 57, 86, 126, 129, 137, 175-176
Spinning Jenny 85
Static cost sheet 176
Stern Report 147-148, 151
Strategic supplier 42-45, 115, 176
Structural .... v, 57, 59, 125, 176
Subcontractor .... xiv, 8-9, 111, 176
Subscription-based retailers 153
Supplier side ..... xii, xiv-xv, 13, 37, 75, 77, 101, 103, 105, 125, 142, 165, 176
Supply chain ...xv, 54, 73, 75, 81, 89, 110, 116, 127, 129, 132-133, 138, 150, 153, 157, 170, 176
Sustainability 37-38, 60, 75, 102, 111, 113, 148, 170, 174, 176
Sweatshop 102, 111, 142, 167, 176
Systemic 57, 125, 176
T-shirt .... xiv, 4, 8, 19, 34, 44, 50-51, 63, 126
Target 23, 50, 66, 79, 81-82, 86, 108, 115-116, 172-173
Tariff 53-54, 143, 170, 172-173, 176
Tazreen 146
ThredUp 159
Toteme 157
Trial orders 57-58, 85-86, 99, 129, 176
Trim .... ix, xiii, 3-5, 7, 11-12, 14-15, 17, 21, 27-30, 44, 46-47, 53, 55, 58, 63-67, 93, 114, 129, 169-170, 172, 175-176
Tukatech .... v, 89, 92
Turkey 18, 47

Index

Twitter 176
Underwear .... xiv, 34, 44, 63, 156
Universal Factory Supplier 101, 115-117, 119-120
Vertical Integration 176
Vietnam 18, 34, 47, 145, 149
Vintage clothing 176
Vinted 159
Walmart 83, 108, 145
Weaving 24, 171
Whole Foods 39
Work in process 6, 149, 170, 173, 176
Work in progress 176
YKK 129, 131-134
Zipper 21-22, 41, 47, 129-134

www.ingramcontent.com/pod-product-compliance
Lightning Source LLC
Chambersburg PA
CBHW051944290426
44110CB00015B/2108